Thanks
----
for the

Memos!

Thanks for the Memos!

Michael Feldman

PETERSON'S/PACESETTER BOOKS

PRINCETON, NEW JERSEY

Visit Peterson's Education Center on the Internet (World Wide Web) at
http://www.petersons.com

Thanks For The Memos! is published by Peterson's/Pacesetter Books.

Pacesetter Books, Peterson's/Pacesetter Books, and the Pacesetter horse are
trademarks of Peterson's Guides, Inc.

Library of Congress Cataloging-in-Publication Data

Feldman, Michael, 1949–
    Thanks for the memos! / Michael Feldman.
      p.   c.
    ISBN 1-56079-523-9
    1. Business writing. 2. Memorandums—Humor. I. Title.
HF5718.3.F45   1995
658.4'53—dc20   95-3269
                                                   CIP

Cover design by Susan Newman
Interior design by Kathy Kikkert
Cover photographs by Anthony Loew

Printed in the United States of America

10 9 8 7 6 5 4 3 2 1

For Ellie and Nora,
still in the wonderful world of play.

Contents

Why Thanks?
Why Memos?

I didn't start out to collect memos. I started out to do radio, which, as of this writing, I'm still starting out to do. The essence of radio is that it takes up a lot of time, all of which must be filled: by music, news, phone calls, weather, banter, and, when banter fails, by filler—little bits from the wire services, *Farmer's Almanac*, listener mail—all in the hopes of avoiding the much dreaded "dead air."

While doing a radio show about twelve years ago at Wisconsin Public Radio in Madison someone sent me a memo from a hospital pathology unit which described the conversion of the men's toilet into a doctor's office and the domino effect it had on the elevator's transformation into the autopsy dressing room. Needless to say, I was hooked: "Thanks for the Memos" was born. Ever since, each week on my Public Radio International show "Whad'ya Know?" I have been reading actual memos sent in by actual listeners, with pertinent names deleted so that actual listeners shall not perish from the earth, or at least that part of it governed by Arbitron.

Since that fateful moment I have received (which is not to say kept, as it quickly begins to get ridiculous) some six or seven thousand memos, photocopies, hand-scrawled signs ripped from doors, items clipped from internal (house) organs, quaint-looking carbons, and cutting-edge e-mail printouts (fears of e-mail eradicating the memo have proved as unfounded as the fears that television would wipe out movies)—making me somewhat of an authority (or at least a repository) in a field that doesn't seem to have many authorities: memology.

Somebody ought to look into it. The number of people who have stashed workplace memos is astonishing and their reasons for doing so might tell you something about the American workplace in the tail end of the twentieth century; you know, hopes, dreams, the whole nine yards. Most are examples of what the recipients regard as being outrageous, insulting, demeaning or absurd: procedures that make no sense, admonitions that could have come from a junior high school vice-principal, worrisome developments threatening the inalienable rights to coffee, two-ply toilet paper, and decorated cubicles, and corporate total quality doublespeak, which makes some want to walk the walk right out the door.

Some of the submitted memos, judging from the attached notes written in lipstick, come from individuals with an ax to grind, but most are examples of "this is just typical" from what appear to be well-adjusted careerists in a wide range of occupations and preoccupations. Over the years, after all, the rank and file have to endure a steady diet of this sort of thing, from a succession of memo writers with varying degrees of skill in motivation and English usage; as a result they get to be pretty knowledgeable critics.

Since these memos are selected by my listeners (in turn selected out by their tendency to listen to public radio) I can't claim that this sample is a scientific overview of the internal concerns of the retail organizations, businesses, corporations, insurance companies, govenment agencies, or universities from which they sprang. They are all, though, amusing for one reason or another and might perhaps serve as models of what to avoid in the art of business communication—although I hope not avoided entirely, as I do have airtime to fill.

Rest assured, all names and company references have been changed or deleted so that the memo writers' positions will not. Otherwise, these memos are intact, uncorrected, and accompanied only by my observations on the not-so-fine art of business memos.

Michael Feldman

Introduction

I'm not in a position to write memos. Well, I'm in a position to write them, but no one is in a position to read them. Therein lies the essence of the business memorandum: there needs to be a hierarchy, a flow chart with somebody to drip on. There are exceptions to the direction of the top-down communique, when, heroically or foolishly, a simple wage-earner leaps salmon-like upriver attempting to spawn a complaint or hatch a policy, but in general it's Mr. Dithers or his quisling hurling the lightning bolt missives, as Zeus might have were he riled up about the unauthorized use of the copier, culottes at the cooler, or the flagrant and dangerous opening of windows. But then again, you don't get to be a god by being petty. Do you?

Are memos a form of communication? Yes, although unlike most models of communication (outside marriage), a reply is not desired, merely the cessation or instigation of activity, a change in outlook or practice, or the spontaneous conversion to the zealotry of Frederick Winslow Taylor, the father of scientific management, who advised workers "your job is to find out what your boss wants and give it to him exactly as he wants."

Issuing a memo is a profoundly idealistic enterprise not unlike those undertaken by Luther or Marx, in that it is based on a tangible belief in the primacy and the power of the word over human nature as revealed by the time-honored qualities of lethargy, habit, fear of change, hostility toward authority, and that old bugaboo, commonsense. The memoist believes in the perfectibility of human nature and that it damn well better happen soon. The fact that so many of their employees save these memos and send them to me indicates the degree to which this idealism may be misplaced.

Memos are X-rays (they are internal, after all) of the men and women who send them, revealing the health and functioning of their dispositions and illuminating their feelings about just what business they believe themselves to be in. Reading this particular collection might even cause an executive or manager to realize that business is, for better or worse, dealing with people and only secondarily producing wire rope.

-1-

Please Make Sure

to Read All My Memos

The Ten Commandments might be considered the archetypical memo, having all the requisites, being, namely, a short, internal directive from on high. Most of the authors of the memos we encounter, of course, don't enjoy the same status as the One whose directives Moses transcribed (and, yes, they were written in stone), although you often wouldn't know it from their prose styles, which tend toward Biblical exhortation, albeit with serious grammatical problems. So, too, many an executive, manager, or supervisor, after issuing edicts, will descend to the factory or office floor to find the rank and file worshipping the Golden Bull. It only goes to show, it's never easy to lord it over people.

Not everyone has a Moses to fend for him or her, either; today's executive typically finds himself or herself trying to communicate directly and decisively to scores of people, often across national and cultural boundaries, without even knowing which end of or whether the office Wang is up or down. Writing in *The New York Times* recently, Peter H. Lewis described a CEO technology retreat where execs intimidated by their own electronic mail could ask Mr. Wang himself when to single-click or double-click the mouse (Wang's rule: "try clicking once, and if nothing happens, click twice.") Within an hour, they had produced a passable two-line e-mail memo, although the knotty issue of content had not been addressed. Within a day the titans of the Fortune 500 had become electronic toddlers and, one can assume, would soon be into everything including cyberspace, until recently the exclusive domain of their computer literate employees who could pretty much do with it as they pleased.

Many companies are only now beginning to realize what's been going on on the Internet; *The Wall Street Journal* reports that Hallmark Cards, for example, one of only 40 percent or so of companies with a policy on electronic mail, warns all e-mail users to "assume the message you send will never be destroyed" (along with your permanent record, now hurtling through cyberspace.)

With the boss logging on, no one is safe. The memo, rather than being rendered obsolete by electronic mail, now is the ghost in the machine, keeping alive admonitions on proper telephone use, inputting self-input forms, and putting forward the six skeletomuscular positions to strike (a kind of office t'ai chi) when attempting to remove a pocket calculator from the viper's pit that is the center desk drawer. Along with ever vigilant Xeroxes, still-to-be-found hand-scrawled glyphs, and proliferating in-house publications, the waterfront is covered.

But, judge for yourself—and please make sure to read all my memos.

MEMO TO:
BRAND-O-GRAM

Please make sure to read <u>all</u> my memos.

Thanks.

_____
Jim Brand
Assembly Foreman

TO: Andrew Philips

FROM: Alice Simon

SUBJECT: Robot Harassment

DATE SENT: 12/01

Hello:

   If you notice anyone annoying, harassing, abusing, or purposefully blocking the path of the ROBOT, please:

1.) Tell them to stop
2.) Get their name (for employees) and/or department
3.) Report them IMMEDIATELY to Me!

I will notify their supervisor (or the Hospital Medical Director for those darn interns and resident physicians) and will call them into my office to SCOLD them.

The ROBOT is an employee of our Department and should be treated with respect. (not to mention that the needless harassment really messes with his mind!!)

Thanks, Alice

The next hot office issue: robot harassment.

MY PERSONAL POLICY REGARDING
***** THE DOOR *****

Since I have two doors to my office, let's dispose of one immediately. The entrance from the hallway, marked Private is not to be used. Frankly it scares me to suddenly have someone appearing over my shoulder, and I'd prefer that this not be used at all.

You are welcome at almost all times through the door from the accounting office. Most of the time that door is open, so that those of you who have papers in my office, may come and go at will. I would appreciate your simply entering, retrieving the papers you need, and leaving by the same door as quietly as you can. If I haven't know you were here, you've done it right.
For those of you who wish to speak to me, the door is open so that you may do so easily. Most of you seem to have little difficulty with this situation, and I'm always happy to hear from you.

IF THE DOOR IS CLOSED, please do NOT knock. At times I will close the door to afford a bit more quiet, or to hold a quiet conversation, BUT AT NO TIME DOES THE CLOSED DOOR MEAN YOU SHOULD NOT ENTER. What you should not do is knock. Please come in, and act as if the door was open before you turned the knob.
IF THE DOOR IS CLOSED AND THE KNOB DOES NOT TURN, IT IS LOCKED. . . . DON'T KNOCK UNLESS YOUR SITUATION IS CRITICAL. The locked door means that I'd like to remain undisturbed, and prefer not to be interrupted. If you knock I will stop what I am doing and leave my chair and go over to the door and open it to see what it is you have that is critical. I truly hope it is.
Please try to understand that I'd like to be forever available, but that there are times when I simply can not be.

Fortunately, there are only two doors to his office. What do you say we get maintenance up here and weld 'em shut?

August 2
MEMORANDUM

To: All Staff

From: Donald Roberts

re: Scandal mongering and television watching

It has come to my attention that scandalous rumors about the personal lives of various individuals in our Association continue to be circulated among the staff and other organizations in this building. This is intolerable and is particularly distressing in view of the efforts that have been made over the past several years to address and control rumors, to deal with the damage done by the spreading of scandalous rumors, and (most recently) to incorporate clear guidance on the subject in the new personnel handbook.

I am struck by the coincidence of the rise in scandalous gossip and the practice over the past few years of some members of the staff watching soap operas on the television during the lunch hour. This practice was disapproved of by the Acting Executive Director, who nevertheless tolerated it because he believed it had no effect outside one private office during the lunch hour; that in particular no members or "customers" would be aware of, or otherwise put off by, the practice. I am now of the opinion that its effects are not contained, that it predisposes some staff members to salacious concerns, and that it must be ended.

Therefore, effective immediately and until further notice, the following policies will be in effect:

1. There will be no use of the television, except for the watching of videos on subjects encompassed within the long range plan, without permission from a member of the senior management team.

(continues)

2. There will be no watching of any television in the offices during the normal work week without permission from a member of the senior management team.

All staff, whether they formerly watched soap operas or not, are reminded that we expect courteous and respectful behavior at all times. I am hopeful that the curtailment of soap opera watching, the disciplining of involved staff members, and this reminder of our policy will serve to remedy the current situation. I also believe that most members of the staff share my gratitude to those who helped bring this matter to a conclusion and my hope that we will now all work together, cheerfully and cooperatively, to put this most recent episode behind us.

Welcome to "The Young and the Unemployed"

INTER-OFFICE MEMORANDUM

TO: ALL ASSOCIATES

DATE: 8/18

FROM: Keri Mark

RE: MEAL RELIEF PERIODS AND TIME CLOCK USE

Through obervations over the last several months it has become clear that we have a serious and widespread abuse of meal relief periods. Specifically, we have observed the practice of spending substantial amounts of time when travelling from work areas to the lounge and the practice of punching in from a meal relief and returning to a table and resuming a seat and/or conversation for substantial amounts of time.

Plain and simply, the practices described above constitute time theft and are equivalent to stealing from the company. Obviously, any of us who engages in this kind of wilful and deliberate behavior is placing her/his job in very serious jeopardy. In fact, this is among the violations of policy described in the "Welcome Book" as possibly leading to immediate termination.

Let me share with you some examples of this conduct, so that we may all achieve a clear understanding of this problem and its solution.

Examples:

Associate A departs her/his work area for lunch and travels slowly through the lower level stopping to talk with several associates along the way.

Ten minutes later, she/he steps on the escalator en route to the lounge. Upon arriving at the lounge, she/he immediately ducks into the restroom for 5 minutes.

(continues)

On coming out of the restroom, the associate then proceeds to the refrigerator to pickup her/his lunch. Then she/he goes to the microwave to prepare her/his lunch for 3 minutes.

Meal Relief Periods and Time Clock Use

At this point, having set her/his lunch at a table, the associate walks to the timeclock and punches out for lunch noting her/his out punch as 12:40 P.M.

Later. . . .

At exactly 1:25 P.M., the associate punches in, then proceeds into the restroom for 5 minutes and returns to the table to clear her/his lunch utensils plus strikes up a conversation with one of her/his tablemates which goes on for 5 minutes.

Now let's assume this practice by this one associate occurs only once a week. The total time off the floor and not punched out amounts to 33 minutes. Let's establish that reasonable travel time to and from the associates work area ranges between 5–10 minutes. That leaves 23 minutes of unauthorized time. Let's consider an annual calculation of that time:

23 minutes × 52 weeks = 19.93 hours per yr.

First of all, our casual observation shows this behavior is rampant and not occasional. Also, all the on-floor conversations serve to distract working associates from serving customers. As well, this behavior disrupts the lunch hours of others and causes lapses of coverage on the floor. This problem has been observed on both the lower and upper levels.

Please be advised that this conduct will not be tolerated and will be cause for disciplinary action should these practices continue.

Thank you for your cooperation.

Why omniscience comes in handy in the retail trade.

Dear Market Supporter,

Our mid-winter informational Seminar was a success! Thanks for your help.

Plan to attend our next meeting on March 21.

MEMO to Growers: Thank you for your participation. We look forward to more vendors, more rain and more customers next year. The Market appreciates your vegetable produce in all its wondrous variety. However, it has come to the Coordinator's attention that some vegetables with odd shapes have been displayed prominently to consumers just looking for average produce. While gardeners may be pre-occupied with reproductive functions, it seems the Associate Mayor and unnamed elderly female patrons of our market are NOT!

THEREFORE: in the future growers will be prohibited from flaunting their misshapen eggplants, peppers, tomatoes, kohlrabi or any other vegetables with indentations or proturberances that suggest human anatomy IN ANY SHAPE OR FORM.

The painting of cleavage, "happy faces", private hair and other physical representations will also BE DISCOURAGED! Commencing immediately, the Coordinator will strictly enforce standards of public decency appropriate to our citizens.

Clean up or cull your questionable vegetables! While you may continue to sell such produce under the table or out of the truck, the City Council recommends it stay out of sight. The Coordinator will deal with infractions IMMEDIATELY with a PARING KNIFE. Second violators will be warned verbally, a third offense will lead to a two-week banishment from our market.

Please put your garden "curiousities" on the compost pile, thanks.

Sincerely,

Coordinator

From a farmer's market association — word of some really fresh produce.

INTEROFFICE COMMUNICATION

TO: Team Members
DATE: December 1
FROM: Human Resources
RE: Chain Letters

Please duplicate this and send it to six others you want to have good luck.

DEFINE THE SITUATION

Chain letters have been appearing within inter-office mail in increasing numbers. This is strictly prohibited by company policy. A chain letter sent through the U.S. Mail is illegal (Title 18 U.S.C. 1302).

PLAN THE SOLUTION

All team members are asked to adhere to company policy and to advise their team members of the PONC involved in writing, copying and mailing such letters in our quality conscious environment.

THE FIX

There is no need to implement a temporary fix if all team members adhere to policy and become a part of the solution.

IDENTIFY THE ROOT CAUSE

Superstitions that bad things will happen if chain letters are not forwarded are causing additional unwarranted work in the mail rooms and PONC in offices and copying rooms.

CORRECTIVE ACTION

Team members should adhere to policy and stop sending chain letters through inter-office mail and utilizing other company resources for supply and distribution. Any failure to adhere should be regarded as cause for corrective disciplinary action up to, and including, discharge.

TO: Legal Staff

RE: Office Absences

For those of you who missed the presentation on this new procedure: if you are going to be absent for any reason you should call anyone in Legal who will be absent at the same time and that person must call a third person who is not absent but promises not to tell anybody (particularly me) about either absence unless such third person overhears any fourth or fifth parties discussing whether you are absent. We think this new procedure should ensure that the least amount of information concerning your whereabouts will reach the least amount of people in the most amount of time, utilizing the most amount of people. It should work. However, if there is any possible way to communicate less information to less people using more time and people, please feel free to make a recommendation. I think we've made real progress.

Finally, a policy that reflects reality!

Memo

To: Michael

From: Serena

Date: October 11   *Plan accordingly!*

Re: PMS

The following is a list of names and the time of the month that PMS usually occurs:

<u>1st Week of the Month</u>
Carol—therefore no pay checks will be cut that week, please
        budget accordingly
Sara —She gets it bad
Janet

<u>2nd Week of the Month</u>
Marcy—if you think she's grumpy now, wait till this week!
Ada
Bonnie

<u>3rd Week of the Month</u>
Karen
Daniella
Ronnie

<u>4th Week of the Month</u>
Inga   Joanne
Gerry   Donna
Jamie   Beverly
Angela   Karen
Esther   Alice
Margaret

You may want to consider calling in sick yourself during this week.

MEMO

TO: Business Staff

FROM: Renee Maple

DATE: March 18

RE: Reception Desk

I have been asked to remind everyone answering
the telephone and greeting guests to please be
more careful of their language.

Apparently, at least one unnamed business staff
person is in the habit of swearing out loud when
interrupted . . . for example, the phone rings
and the person says ''D - - n'' and then answers
the phone.

If this applies to you, then please stop.

*The telephone - what do you do
when it makes that noise and
you have only a few seconds
to react? Many are called, but
a few have chosen the wrong
response.*

```
To:        Therapy Staff

From:      Ellen

Date:      12/7/93
```

I first want to say how much I love and
appretiate each of you. If I didn't love you, it
would be hard to say the following; but because
I do, I must, even tho it is difficult.

It has come to my attention that one or more
of you is regularly passing gas in the inner
office.

Please stop it! This is not a joke! That is a
small area; it has poor ventilation; and it
causes problems for those working in there.

Peg did not bring this to my attention. They
do not know of this memo, and I prefer it not be
discussed with them. If you want (or need) to
discuss this with me (especially if it is your
problem), I will do so. (Gas or flatulence
indicates GI problems, you may want to discuss
this with your doctor).

Thanks for helping out.

Two examples (see the next memo)
of a problem as old as man himself: the first stateside, the
second from Saudi Arabia,
where "William" was soon
blowing in the wind.

Date <u>12th November</u>

To: William Carver

From: Kamal Ahmad

I am writing to express my dis-satisfaction with your behaviour when you called into this office on 12 November at 14.30 hours.

You were talking to Sam with Ikko Yoshimo present when you expelled an unusually audible anal discharge of intestinal gas. This is very offensive particularly to an Asian and Sam felt sufficiently embarrased as to leave his own office. This is the second occasion I have known you to behave in such a manner.

This memo is to be kept on file and if there should be cause for any furhter disciplinary action concerning your behaviour you will be dismissed without notice and benefits.

Resident Manager

ALL CR PERSONNEL

DISABLING INJURY

We have experienced a lost time disabling injury. On Wednesday, November 18, an employee reached into the center drawer of his desk from a standing position to retrieve a pocket calculator. He experienced a "twinge" in his back but the event did not seem serious at the time. The next morning he experienced acute lower back pain and unable to get out of bed. The employee missed a total of 3 days work. Since at least one full day of work was missed this is classified as a disabling injury per the OSHA reporting standards.

The purpose of keeping statistics and rewarding performance based on those statistics is to promote safe working conditions and practices. It is the safety of employees and not records that is the goal. It is unfortunate our record of more than three years without a loss time disabling injury was broken. We can take solace in the fact, however, that the injury did not result from an ominous safety condition or act. In this case the weight of the upper body when angled produced the load on the back. This highlights the vulnerability of the back and hopefully will reinforce the need to employ correct lifting procedures at all times. This will be especially true during the continuing consolidation as employees not normally engaged in such activity are called on to lift or move equipment and/or materials. If engaged in such activities, please remember to:

- Keep your back straight and use your legs; leg muscles are stronger than back muscles.

- Avoid unnecessary bending.

- Avoid twisting your spine.

- Avoid reaching; get close to the load and hold it close.

(continues)

- Avoid too much weight; get help with big loads.

- Avoid jerking; a sudden pull can double the strain.

Our Safety Clock will reappear after the first of the year, set to zero. Missing will be number of FIRST AID cases. In its place will be OFF THE JOB INJURIES. Management wants to encourage greater safety awareness away from the work place. More employees are injured and more time lost in off the job accidents than at work.

Enjoy a safe and happy holiday.

Hard to believe in three years nobody reached for his pocket calculator. Then the guy goes and falls off the ladder — resetting the safety clock.

August 28, 1986

To: Lars Nolan, Benjamin Dean, Hank Crowley

From: Mike Andrews

Subject: <u>American Work Ethic</u>

On Ellis Island stands the Statue of Liberty. This proud symbol of our national heritage has presided over the entrance to this energetic land of generations of immigrants who have forged the bounty around us from the rich supply of dreams for a brighter tomorrow. The product of this dream has been a surging and relentless pulse as of one great entity of which we, as men, are but parts. It carries us forward on a tide of achievement with pride, accomplishment with resolve, and pizza with Cola-Cola. This dream though carries a responsibility which begins with starting our appointed jobs at the appointed times.

In the future, please be sure to adjust the start time on your time cards to reflect occassions when 3:30 p.m. finds your motovational reserves at a low ebb. It is my hope that your motivational reserves will never be at a low ebb at 3.30 p.m. and further that my hopes will never be turned to dispair. Remember: "When duty whispers low, "thou must", the youth replies, "I can". If you can't begin at 3:30 regularly, see me for attitude adjustment.

Dispensed by a vending machine company, some faulty directions to the Statue of Liberty (she's on Liberty Island, and is French to boot). In the beverage industry youth replies, "I can!"

To   All Staff

Subject   National Meeting

Dictated by   SL/bl

Re. Yours of

Date   11/29   .

It has been brought to our attention that even though the company will <u>NOT</u> be able to pay for your spouses to go to Lake Tahoe, some of you are trying and planning to have them attend at your own expense. Due to the arrangements that have been made (airport transportation/tickets, group activities, meetings, etc., etc.) we do not see how or where you would have any time to spend with them. Every day from the day you arrive until the day you leave, (excluding Thursday) we have activities planned as a group, from 9:00 A.M. until at least 10:00 P.M. We believe that any spouses attending would only be distracting to our National Sales Meeting.

Please be aware that <u>ALL</u> air travel, hotel accommodations and group activities ARE etched in stone as a group, with absolutely <u>NO CHANGES</u> possible. We are sorry that we can not accommodate any of your spouses in Lake Tahoe. Bottomline is; if you continue your quest and it interferes with our National Sales Meeting plans in any way (OUR sole discretion), disciplinary action will follow.

Don't worry, be happy, next year we're planning to go to; Minot, North Dakota, so we won't have any of these problems.

Taking spouses? Come on, people!

To: Newsroom staff

From: Janet Brower

Subject: Pens

Until some weeks ago, more than $100 a week of
our newsroom budget was being spent on pens. We
were averaging around $120 or so. That's a few
dollars more than $500 a month.

I'm sure you'd all agree that spending that much
on pens is excessive.

We certainly want to provide everyone with all
the tools they need to do their jobs. We'd
simply like to spend a little less on pens, and
would ask that you help us, just by being aware,
that's all.

I asked my assistant to round up renegade pens
and writing utensils; this was not a directive
to hand over your extras. But now those are in
the supply cabinet, which we will continue to
keep stocked.

I'm not altogether sure it would be a bad idea if fewer reporters had pens, but I guess that's not the same as reporters having fewer pens.

TO:	All Court House Staff	DATE:	10/11
FROM:	Carol	RE:	SCENTS

This is a plea to everyone regarding a problem we have here that is reoccuring. We have at least four people on our staff who have respiratory or other problems with odors/scents/smoke, etc. Our problems and symptoms vary but include things like nausea, migraine headaches, increasing asthma medication, and sore throats. Others have fewer symptoms but are none the less impacted by strong scents.

We plead with all of you to keep this in mind. If you must wear a cologne/perfume/after shave or other scent, please keep it to a bare minimum. Others should not be able to smell it when you walk by or walk into their work area.

If you use the restrooms, please use only matches to get rid of odors and do not dose the room up with air fresheners (burn one match and then dispose of it in the toilet, NOT THE TRASH CONTAINER). When you leave the restroom others have offices near them and do not have the advantage of "leaving" the scents. Natural scents dissipate much quicker than the air fresheners.

As to the asthma irritants, it is very important not to use aerosal sprays in my vicinity (eg. the restrooms). That includes hair spray, anti static sprays, lysol, etc. Pump sprays are OK if used very lightly so the scents don't linger or spread into the hallways.

If you have just smoked a cigarette, wait at least 10 or 15 minutes before you talk to someone else at close range (eg. less than 4 feet from their breathing space . . .). Same goes for eating strong smelling food items or drinking coffee.

Some of us may suffer for many hours AFTER work when exposed to such irritants. Please help us and forgive us our weaknesses!

Yet another hot office issue — Second hand smells. (Speaking of irritating . . .)

Date: January 8

To: Development Computer Center Users
Department: See Distribution

From: A. D. Grant
Department: Development Computer Center
Phone: 1784

Subject: User Request Procedures

In the past we had many complaints about user notification, or lack thereof, as we neglected to inform you as to what we were going to do with your requests, when you could expect to see them completed, and when they were actually completed. These complaints were justified, so we tried to do something to improve the situation. We developed a procedure for the User Request Form which is designed to provide the necessary service.

If, as indicated on the form, you fill out and send the entire form to us, you will receive the pink copy after someone is assigned to the project and a reasonable completion date is determined. Unfortunately, many of you want a copy for yourselves, but don't want to make one on a copier; so you take the gold copy, which is supposed to be our file copy, off the back. When this happens, we use the pink copy for our file copy. Then the person assigned has no copy to send back to you for your information.

As long as you persist in taking our file copy, we will use your "Originator" copy for our file. If you want a copy to keep when you first send in the request, you can make it. We are not going to do it for you. I do not want to hear any complaints about not getting notification in this case. You will continue to get the yellow response copy when we are finished with the task.

We will appreciate your cooperation & support.

Two examples (see the next memo) of the tenuous relationship between form and function.

REQUEST, TURN-IN AND RECEIPT FOR
PROPERTY OR SERVICES

TO: Supply Officer	REQUESTING OFFICE *Anesthesiology Service*				
CITATION REQUESTED ☐ DELIVERY ☐ TURN-IN	DATE PREPARED *4/13*		DATE REQUIRED *4/15*		
ITEM NO. OR STOCK NO. *(If available)*	DESCRIPTION	QUAN- TITY	UNIT	EST. UNIT COST	

Repair IBM Wheelwriter
6 typewriter
Typewriter is in
Room 5085 (5w).
See Mary Amar in
Room 5085 for details.

JUSTIFICATION OF NEED OR TURN-IN *(If recurring need, indicate 30 day estimate. If turn-in, do not use this form if circumstances require use of form 9101712. Report of Survey)*

Typewriter is jammed in its start-up
phase when power is turned on . all lights go on, a
whir is heard, then no change.

SIGNATURE OF INITIATOR *Sally Stadro*	SIGNATURE OF APPROVING OFFICIAL *Chief Anesthesiology Serv.*	DATE *4/13*

ROUTING SLIP

TO *(Name or title — Mail routing symbol)*	INITIALS — DATE
1. 125 ANESTHESIOLOGY	
2. 90B	
3.	

REMARKS
THIS REQUEST NEEDS TO BE TYPEWRITTEN FOR
SUBMISSION TO 90B

FROM 90B	DATE 4/13

NOTICE

(1) Please refrain from leaving undergarments or sports gear in or around the lavatory facilities. It can be very dangerous, as I'm sure you'll all remember.

Last month Mrs. Wicker tripped on a piece of male undergarment and bruised her leg, and Mr. Lincor fell over someone's running shoe left in the corridor and bumped his head on the lavatory facility.

These and other lavatory accidents can be avoided if we are careful with our undergarments and sports equipment.

(2) If the liquid soap dispenser evidences a low level, please do not attempt to open it from the top. Serious injury could result from residual soap pressure build-up in the jar. Tape a note to the dispenser explaining the problem or, better yet, call the custodian for help. His name is Carlo, and make sure you call him by name to insure prompt service.

(3) We are again experiencing complaints from many workers about loud singing and shrieking from employees while in the locker room shower.

As we discussed at last month's meeting, loud singing or screaming are discouraged, although humming or singing at a low volume is permissible.

Please try to effect all the aforementioned directives to insure all of us a safe, happy and healthy new year.

Thanks in advance for your cooperation.

In fairness, how many of us over the years have tangled with female undergarments?

Office Memorandum

DEPARTMENT   State Office of NATURAL RESOURCES

TO: Dan

FROM: Mark

SUBJECT: PARTS IS PARTS

I need a legal opinion from the Attorney Generals office. The question is whether a whitetail's penis is part of the hide and therefore legal to buy/sell, or part of the carcass and illegal to buy/sell; although I realize it depends upon the skinning technique. The local chapter was approached by an individual who claims to have a very lucrative market for these parts among Hmong and oriental locations overseas. He claims that each one could fetch as much as $250.00, which could generate considerably more dollars although we have not yet come up with a sociably acceptable slogan. Please advise.

If not "Hides for "Habitat," perhaps "Penises for Preservation"?

INTERDEPARTMENTAL CORRESPONDENCE

To: All Supervision   cc: Date: December 10
From: K. S. Surba
Subject: Cleanliness Requirements in Soldering Areas

Process Engineering has been tasked with providing an interpretation of our policy manual on Cleanliness. Sentence number three of this paragraph states:

> "Eating, smoking, or drinking at a work station
> shall be prohibited."

Based on the training received by plantside Category C Solderability Experts, the interpretation of this paragraph shall not include the prohibition of chewing gum as a form of eating. However, to comply with cleanliness requirements in the work area and to protect the integrity of the hardware, the following guidelines shall be followed when chewing gum at work stations:

1. The chewing gum shall be unwrapped and placed into the mouth prior to entering the work area and prior to applying protective devices (fingercots or gloves).

2. The chewing gum shall remain in the mouth at all times while in the work area.

3. The chewing gum must be disposed of outside of the work area.

These guidelines shall serve as the minimum requirements. Area supervision may enforce stricter requirements as deemed necessary. This clarification shall be incorporated into our policy.

Next they'll be regulating Godliness in the soldering areas. (The "shall's" are already in place.)

-2-

Conjugating
Our Resources

I n *The Elements of Style* (Macmillan, 1979), E. B.
White cites William Strunk Jr. as having summarized
the qualities of good writing as follows:

> Vigorous writing is concise. A sentence should contain no
> unnecessary words, a paragraph no unnecessary sentences, for
> the same reason that a drawing should have no unnecessary
> lines and a machine no unnecessary parts. This requires not
> that the writer make all his sentences short, or that he avoid all
> detail and treat his subjects only in outline, but that every
> word tell. (p.xiv)

For the most part, the only rule the following memos
observe is that many of the words are telling. But what?
That "a significant cost avoidance was . . . realized," that a
"policy on policy (interim)" has been established, and the

admission that "sometimes we could create more of a problem by sharing information." Before our very eyes, we see verbs conjugated in the past perfect tense, double negatives negated, and a long overdue counterattack on the "proliferation of syllables." Lovers of legalese will appreciate *et. seq.* being cleared up once and for all, and weather buffs will glean the latest on the probability of precipitation (and the probability that any clarification of the forecast will remain cloudy). For managers or just people-persons looking to dish out positive reinforcement, there are "50 ways to say 'You're Great!'" while those of you who love a mystery will relish contemplating why three ladies were riding up and down the elevator for 48 hours. All this and the unexpected uses of copulation at the veterinary hospital, too!

Although "It's only words," as the Bee Gees so wisely put it, "words are all we have." Sense—why, that's another word entirely, unless it's a sense of history and culture: consider the gong, traced from Hsi Yu (between Tibet and Burma) in 500 A.D. to a midwest regional loan office where it now rings out the Second Millennium in the spiritual quest for loan payoffs and property sales. (A Zen master might wordlessly cut a loan officer in half for really special occasions.)

In short, some turn phrases and some have phrases turn on them—but that's the price we pay when "conjugating our resources."

Interoffice Memo

To		Date	November 12
From	Dept	Re	<u>Recognition</u>

On myriad occasions we have conjugated our resources to focus on the global needs of the corporation. As a result, we have achieved goals that might have otherwise been unattainable

I personally thank you for your collective efforts in facilitating our environmental operations last week. By availing equipment and manpower, sixteen dump trailers were promptly loaded with soil for disposal. Your assistance was particularly crucial, since we were under considerable time constraints, precipitated by dynamic corporate needs. Furthermore, a significant cost avoidance was also realized.

This effort is indicative of continuous improvement in its purest form, and is synonymous with the concept of teamwork. Utilizing a concert of expertise and resources by crossing departmental demarcations can truly benefit the totality.

Please convey my thanks to all personnel who contributed to this endeavor. I applaud them for their consideration and exemplary performance.

Thanks again for you continued cooperation.

Some toxic prose from the toxic waste people.

TO: ALL OFFICES
            DOMESTIC DATA SERVICE USERS

FROM: CHIEF, SERVICES DEVELOPMENT BRANCH

SUBJECT: NEW EQUATIONS FOR THE NGM-BASED MOS
            PROBABILITY OF PRECIPITATION (POP)
            FORECAST

EFFECTIVE WITH THE 1200 UTC CYCLE ON SEPTEMBER
9, THE NGM-BASED MOS PROBABILITY OF PRECIPITATION
(POP) AVAILABLE IN THE FWC PRODUCT ON AFOS (ALSO
KNOWN AS FOUS14) WILL BE GENERATED BY NEW
FORECAST EQUATIONS. IN TESTING ON INDEPENDENT
DATA, THE NEW NGM-BASED MOS FORECASTS WERE
GENERALLY MORE ACCURATE THAN EITHER THE OLDER
NGM-BASED MOS OR THE CURRENT LFM-BASED MOS
GUIDANCE. THE IMPROVEMENT IN THE NGM MOS
GUIDANCE WAS PRIMARILY DUE TO THE INCREASED SIZE
OF THE DATA SAMPLE USED TO DEVELOP THE
EQUATIONS. THE DEVELOPMENTAL PROCEDURES WERE
VERY SIMILAR TO THOSE DESCRIBED IN TECHNICAL
PROCEDURES BULLETIN (TPB) NO. 387, ENTITLED "NGM-
BASED MOS GUIDANCE FOR MAXIMUM/MINIMUM
TEMPERATURE, PROBABILITY OF PRECIPITATION, CLOUD
AMOUNT, AND SURFACE WIND." THIS SAME TPB ALSO
DESCRIBES THE FWC PRODUCT AND LISTS THE 204
STATIONS FOR WHICH THE FWC IS GENERATED. IN THE
CURRENT FWC MESSAGE, THE POP FORECASTS ARE
VALID FOR 12-H PERIODS. EQUATIONS TO PRODUCE NGM
MOS FORECASTS OF POP FOR 6-H PERIODS HAVE ALSO
BEEN DEVELOPED, BUT THE GUIDANCE FROM THESE
EQUATIONS IS NOT AVAILABLE AT THIS TIME.
FORECASTERS ARE REFERRED TO TPB 387 FOR A
COMPLETE DESCRIPTION OF THE FWC MESSAGE. A TPB
DESCRIBING THE NEW MOS POP EQUATIONS WILL BE
FORTHCOMING SOON.

(continues)

THE EQUATIONS BEING IMPLEMENTED ARE PART OF A
LARGER EFFORT TO INCREASE THE FORECAST
PROJECTIONS, ELEMENTS, AND STATIONS FOR WHICH
NGM-BASED MOS GUIDANCE PRODUCTS ARE AVAILABLE
TO THE FORECASTER. EFFORTS ARE CURRENTLY
UNDERWAY TO DISSEMINATE THE NEW GUIDANCE TO
THE FIELD. WE EXPECT A NEW FWC MESSAGE TO BE
IMPLEMENTED IN THE FALL. A TPB DESCRIBING THE NEW
MESSAGE SHOULD BE AVAILABLE BY THE END OF
SEPTEMBER.

*All I want to know is,
is it going to rain
or isn't it?*

<u>Memorandum</u>

From: GM

To: Attorneys

Date: September 24

I have an appointment with a neurosurgeon scheduled for Monday which I must cancel. If anyone can use the appointment, please let me know as soon as possible.

Also, I have two tickets available for this Saturday's game. If anyone is interested, please see me.

I think I'll take the tickets.

December 9

MEMO

To: Brad Narrows

From: Rich Harris

This memo is directed to the Maintenance Staff.

Without being sarcastic, I'm wondering why the three ladies that are going down to Southern Copy Roll are riding up and down on the elevator for at least 48 hours. They go up — they go down — but they never get over to Shipping to put the things into a box to be shipped out of town.

Rod, can you please have a daily meeting with the Staff to ask them what possible services can be provided to get things moving? This is absolutely beyond my wildest nightmares that we can be so oblivious to something that takes only a little effort and a little coordination to get off the elevator, and onto the loading dock.

A typo — but one that works!

MRO Gong Celebration

THE GONG

HISTORY

Gongs belong to the oldest and most important musical instruments of South East Asia. Their origins may be traced back to the second millenium B.C., but it is assumed that the gong is much older. In Chinese history gongs are mentioned around 500 A.D., attributed to a nation called HSI YU between Tibet and Burma during the reign of Emperor Hsuan Wu.

Only a few families knew the tradition of gong making as it was passed from generation to generation. The art of making gongs was veiled in a sense of magic. The gong was an important element in the lives of Far East people and it still is in some countries today. In Asian families the gong was an attribute of wealth and served as a status symbol. In rites the gong was used in the evocation of ghosts and in the banning of demons. Touching a gong brought you fortune and strength.

CRAFTING THE GONG

Creating gongs is a dedication to the deeper meaning of the structured, focused vibrations which unfold into sound upon playing the gong and thus have an effect on human beings.

The sound of a gong is created through the skillful craft of the gong maker, guided by his intuitively experienced sound conception. The gong maker begins with a round disc of bronze alloy containing a sound potency which is as of yet still resting within itself; it can then be shaped into frequency ranges and expressions of sound. The tools

(continues)

are fire, steel, hammer, and anvil. He works the alloy until the desired sound becomes alive and can be experienced.

The gong maker has an intensive intuitive conception of the sound
(highs-lows-character-color-expression-impression); a goal therefore, an intent to fulfill this conception.

MIDWEST REGIONAL OFFICE GONG CELEBRATION

As the craftsman of your portfolio consider the gongmaker; his intuition, his conception, his creativity, his patience, his precision.

We will ring the gong to celebrate accomplishments; the completion of a lease, a loan restructuring, a loan payoff, the sale of a property or other outstanding achievements. The person who accumulates the most rings by the end of the year will receive special recognition and a to-be-announced award or bonus.

Ring On!!!

Consider the Gong Show. (Sorry about that premature ring!)

From: Scott 10/8 10:31AM (1520 bytes: 27 ln)

Subject: Use of the word "usage".

- - - - - - - - Message Contents - - - - - - - - -

It is in the interest of every person who must manipulate words
that the unnecessary proliferation of syllables be avoided.
Examples: preventive vs. preventative; orient vs. orientate. This
trend toward a increase in syllables with an accompanying
decrease in clarity is discouraging. Awareness is the best tool in
the battle against the polysyllabic fog which threatens to
smother lucid prose.

   The word "usage" is one of those words which stops the flow
of understanding in one's reading, causes one to stop and ask,
"What does this mean?" Life is short. Recent pieces in cc:mail
have referred to "credit card usage" and "software usage". How
about "credit card use" and "software use" instead?

   I realize this is a small point, but the river of language flows
more smoothly when we choose clarity over muddle. Those of
us in the Corps work to clarify the waters of the United States
under the Clean Water Act. Let us support the clarity of our
language as well by keeping the "Clean English Act" in mind as
we type our way through our daily work.

The next few memos offer some thoughts on grammar, syntax, and usage from various fields of endeavor, underscoring the fact that "awareness is the best tool in the battle against the polysyllabic fog which threatens to smother lucid prose."

To: Staff

Date: November 5

Subject: Definition of "Competent Person"

It has come to my attention that there was some confusion about the definition of "competent person" used in my letter about proper shoring techniques. The definition of a "competent person", taken from the OSHA standard, is as follows: *"A Competent Person means one who is capable of identifying existing and predictable hazards in the surroundings, or working conditions which are unsanitary, hazardous, or dangerous to employees, and who has authorization to take prompt corrective measures to eliminate them."*

According to OSHA, a "competent person" must inspect excavations on a daily basis. At the present time, we do not have any people in our divisions that are trained to meet the criterion set by OSHA. Therefore, the training group is working on a training program for "competent persons".

No offense.

MARCH 14

TO: ALL DATA PROCESSING PERSONNEL

FROM: Mary Rhodes, DATA PROCESSING

THE VERB "TO RUN"

Here is a typical conversation in the Machine Room during a test that requires coordination of jobs:

Programmer: "Has my job ran yet?"

Operator: "Let me check. Yes, it was ran 15 minutes ago."

Software Analyst: "Well, when it was ran, it slowed down the whole system."

When you read the above conversation, you probably noticed that the wrong form of the verb "to run" was used in each sentence. Because this error is made so often in our shop, many of us fail to notice the mistake. It is a fact that using words over and over again in an incorrect way tends to make them sound correct. It is also a fact that grammatical errors are "catching" just like a cold. After hearing words used incorrectly, orally, the same mistakes seem to be made in writing, too. That is why I was asked to write this memo about how to use the verb "to run."

The verb "to run" is most frequently used incorrectly when it is paired with a helping verb. Here are some examples of how the verb "to run" should be used:

"Your job has run."   "Your job will have run."
"Your job will be run."   "Has my job been run?"
"My job should be run first." "My job should have been run."

(continues)

Notice that in all instances when there is a helping verb (have, has, will, should, be, etc.), the correct form of the verb is "run". You do not have to memorize a lot of rules - just remember that if there is a helping verb, always use "run", not "ran".

The only time you should use "ran" is when the sentence is simple past tense and there is no helping verb. Here are examples:

"I ran your job."   "The job ran on time."

Now, here are five sentences. Write in the correct form of the verb "to run". Answers are on the back.

1. My job will be _____ tonight, won't it?

2. The big job _____ very quickly.

3. Your job should be _____ on time.

4. I _____ your job at 10:00.

5. Has John Doe's job _____ yet?

MEMORANDUM

TO: ALL PERSONS MAKING WRITTEN
COMMUNICATIONS DIRECTED OUTSIDE OUR
ORGANIZATION

FROM: Director of communications

SUBJECT: Proper use of theatre and theater

DATE: 12 JULY

We have a problem of communications; it is simply this: many of you do not respect the proper use of the word theatre or understand when it is proper to use the form theater. Particular care needs to be taken when writing letters, memoranda, **press releases**, or other material which will be seen by persons outside our organization.

The form theatre is used to indicate legitimate theatre. It is used for live drama, musical theatre, opera, vaudeville, operetta, dance, (except clogging and square dance,) Classical or jazz concerts and other proper entertainments.

The form theater is used for the vulgar forms of entertainment such as: cinema, cabaret burlesque; rock, country and gospel concerts; political events and, rarely, religious happenings.

Theatre is never associated with mayhem for the sake of violence, such as: boxing, wrestling, British soccer fans, clog dancing, theater of war, theater nuclear weapon(s). In fact you should avoid using either form of the word if politely possible.

Neither the form theatre or theater should be used in respect to television except in unusual cases. When applicable, and please restrict your enthusiasm to the form theater.

(continues)

The form to use when describing a performance space must take into account the qualities of the space and the type of presentation the space is suitable for. A space suitable only for projected presentation is of course a theater; as is a space that is dead hung, thrusts more than one-third, "black box" or "flexible" spaces, arena stages and other similar spaces. Likewise, a theatre has a properly hung gridiron over the stage and thrust, if any. The form theatre also implies proper electrical facilities, good acoustics, adequate dressing rooms, and the other necessities of a good working performance space.

Care should be taken to avoid making errors in identifying "modern" performing spaces; particularly when such spaces are described as: "designed for amplified sound;" usually a cop-out meaning "We don't know nothin' 'bout this here acoustics stuff!" For this reason calling such spaces theatres, (or even theaters,) smacks of obscenity. For instance the Marquis Theatre in New York City, the Sidney Opera House, and the Orange County Performing Arts Center not only have awful acoustics but could probably have a place on the ten ugliest buildings in the world list were it not for the fact that these third rate structures had been designed by such fourth rate individuals that they couldn't commit a first rate ugliness if they had to.

Office Memorandum

DEPARTMENT   REVISOR OF STATE STATUTES

TO: All Personnel

FROM: Rod Petsky

SUBJECT: Et.seq.,etc.

Controversy has arisen over use of the term "et.seq." in the drafting of legislation by our office. An explanation of the origin of the term and its corollary term are perhaps in order at this time.

"Et.seq." is a latin term used in conjunction with a section number, either of state or federal statutes; usually the latter. For instance; 29 U.S.C. section 318, et.seq. The literal translation of the term is: "I don't know where in hell it ends." It should be used only when the draftsperson truly doesn't.

A corollary or perhaps more properly a complimentary term for "et.seq." is the lesser known latin term "st.eeq." (promounced "set eek"). As one might surmise, this term is used when a draftsperson locates what clearly appears to be the ending section in a series and hasn't the foggiest idea as to where the series starts. "St.eeq." translates to; "I don't know where in hell it starts." For instance; 29 U.S.C. section st.eeg.318.

Lest one become confused or worried about the proper use of "et.seq." or "st.eeq.", let me offer a few words of encouragement. Don't worry about misuse of the terms. We have highly placed personnel in other legislative agencies who are there for the purpose of guarding against misuse.

MEMORANDUM

TO: All Staff

FROM: Dean of Student Services

DATE: September 27

SUBJECT: Correct usage of English Grammar for office
           use.

Correct grammar usage of the English language is very important for our offices. It hurts me to be reminded constantly that as a minority people we have failed to be correctly informed and to understand the usage and blending of basic verbs that make up a simple sentence.

I have noticed the following severe wrong usage of the following verbs and tenses:

Verb to Take
Past Perfect Tense

Wrong	Right
I taken . . .	I <u>have</u> taken . . .
You taken . . .	You <u>have</u> taken . . .
He/She or it taken . . .	He/She or it <u>has</u> taken . . .

Plural of Taken

We <u>have</u> taken . . .
You <u>have</u> taken . . .
They <u>have</u> taken . . .

Note: We must always use a helping verb when we use a <u>major verb that is in the past perfect tense such as have.</u> As indicated before, many of us do not understand why we must use a helping verb when <u>we use the past perfect tense when</u> ending (en). Another helping verb that is used is "had".

(continues)

Verb to Take
Past Tense

<u>Wrong</u>	<u>Right</u>
I taken . . .	I <u>took</u> . . .
You taken . . .	You <u>took</u> . . .
He/She or it taken . . .	They <u>took</u> . . .

Verb to See
Past Perfect Tense

<u>Wrong</u>	<u>Right</u>
I seen . . .	I <u>have</u> seen . . .
You seen . . .	You <u>have</u> seen . . .
He/She or it seen . . .	He/She or it <u>has</u> seen . . .

Plural of See

<u>Wrong</u>	<u>Right</u>
We seen . . .	We <u>have</u> seen . . .
You seen . . .	You <u>have</u> seen . . .
He/She or it seen . . .	They <u>have</u> seen . . .

Wrong Sentence Usage

<u>Wrong</u>	<u>Right</u>
He did it heself.	He did it <u>himself</u>.
They did it theyself.	They did it <u>themselves</u>.
They did it theirself.	They did it <u>themselves</u>.

<u>Wrong</u>	<u>Right</u>
I see peoples everyday.	I see <u>people</u> everyday.
She has pretty foots/feets.	She has pretty <u>feet</u>.
They was doing it correctly.	They <u>were</u> doing it correctly.

<u>Wrong</u>	<u>Right</u>
I likes that color.	I <u>like</u> that color.
I see five mens.	I see five <u>men</u>.

(continues)

Double Negative

Wrong	Right
I don't want to do it no more.	I don't want to do it
I does it all the time.	<u>anymore</u>.
	I <u>do</u> it all the time.

Conditional

Wrong	Right
If he was here we could	If he <u>were</u> here we could
get things done.	get things done.
I wish I was with you.	I wish I <u>were</u> with you.

I went to <u>a</u> conference.
(An is used before all nouns that begin with a vowel).

November 7

This memorandum is occasioned by the harsh reminder that one should never make assumptions without a thorough examination of all facets of the issue, and a clear cut assessment of the carefully structured conclusions. To do otherwise is irresponsible. Thusly I have erred.

The misdirection stemmed from an assumption that persons in the business of communication would understand words commonly expressed among English speaking literates.

This, then, will serve as a mini course in remedial reading. Today's lesson will focus on four words with which most of us are acquainted. The definitions of these words finds its authority in Webster's Seventh New Collegiate Dictionary.

PLEASE: Understandably, the comprehension of this word is complicated by the fact that it is not spelled phonetically (PLEEZ). Further, it is sometimes unclear as to who is to be the pleaser, and who is to be the pleasee.

"used to express a polite request"

DON'T: Here, too, potential confusion arises from the fact that it is a contraction of two words, DO NOT. It is generally accepted, however, that the contracted version is more commonly used than the alternative.

"a command or entreaty not to do something"

SLAM: This word is an Anglo-Saxon derivitive of the now archaic Scaninavian word, "slaema." While academicians generally endorse this origin, another theory has been advanced by some who believe that the word dates back to prehistoric ages when a Neanderthal male was observed hurling a large, relatively round rock through a hole, while

(continues)

witnessing cavepersons were heard to utter a tribal-like chant, "slamma jamma do." This hypothesis has been identified as the "Cliff Claven Theory."

"a noisy, violent closing"

DOOR: Historians note that this word actually was recorded in its phonetic spelling in the fourteenth century, before doors were in universal usage. Then, with the greater acceptance of the device, the spoken word was often exaggerated so as to draw emphasis to it. This explains the addition of a second "o" in its official spelling.

"a swinging barrier by which an entry is closed and opened"

As a side note, my recent semi-annual visit to the dentist revealed that my dentures have loosened, as though jarred by some external force.

There is, however, an upside to this situation: the pharmaceutical firm, Bristol Myers Squibb, has extended me their frequent user discount, and has credited me with authoring the Excedrin Headache # 144.

I thank you for your support.

To: All store managers

There must be 50 ways to say ''You're Great!''

If you're looking for a new way to recognize the people you work with, try these phrases on for size. . . .

WOW * way to go * super * outstanding * excellent * great * good work * neat * well done * remarkable * I knew you could do it * I'm proud of you * fantastic * superstar * looking good * bravo * hurray for you * beautiful * now you're flying * you're catching on * you've got it * you're special * you're incredible * hot dog * dynamite * you're unique * nothing can stop you now * good for you * you're a winner * remarkable job * beautiful work * you figured it out * terrific * magnificent * marvelous * what a victory * I admire you * spectacular * great idea * you've discovered something big * you figured it out * you're important * phenomenal * you're my hero * great success * super work * how creative * hip hip hooray * what a good listener * you're fun * you tried hard * you care * you mean a lot to me * you belong * I value your opinion * you've got a friend * I trust you * you make me laugh * you brighten my day * I respect you * I couldn't have done it without you * I like working with you * you just made my day * WOW

To which—on behalf of my toddlers—I would like to add "Super-dee-dooper" and a chorus of "I Love You—You Love Me."

Memorandum

To: All Staff

Date: May 28

File No.: WHC:mle

From: Manager, Employment Development Department

Subject: NOISE ABATEMENT

Recently there has been noted an excessive amount of noise in the office. It is recognized that a certain amount of intercourse is needed between co-workers to provide relief from the demands of our work. However, loud conversation and raucous laughter sometimes interferes with the thought processes of those who are concentrating on their work.

As it states in the office rules: "Excessive noise detracts from the professional appearance of the office. Do not talk across desks; go to the person with whom you need to speak." This is a request that you limit your personal conversation and that you keep it to a "conversational" tone of voice.

I'm sorry, you said " a certain amount of…"?

```
*  *  *  *  *  *  *  *  *  *  *  *  *  *  *  *  *  *  *  *  *  *  *  *
```

DELIVER TO: Brent Moshev

ORIGINAL
SENT: 07/09

TIME: 13:03
FROM: Jacki Bonar
SUBJECT: ERROR IN GUIDELINES PUBLICATIO
PRINT DATE: 07/09   TIME: 13:48

```
*  *  *  *  *  *  *  *  *  *  *  *  *  *  *  *  *  *  *  *  *  *  *  *
```

There is an unfortunate error in the revised Guidelines for the
Cancer-Related Checkup: An Update, Code No. 3402. No, we
are not recommending prostate exams for females. The
correction to the chart on page 9 is being made and will be
distributed as quickly as possible. We are not certain how this
happened but certainly apologize.

It couldn't hurt.

MEMORANDUM

TO: ALL EMPLOYEES
FROM: Lawrence
SUBJECT: POLICING WORK AREAS FOR UPCOMING
            TRADE OPEN HOUSE

This memo will serve as a reminder to all personnel that on Monday, October 12, we will be hosting a couple hundred of our trade contacts to an open house celebration of our 40th anniversary.

Between now and then I would like to ask that everyone set aside a bit of time to police up around their immediate work areas, picking up and organizing that which must be preserved, and subjecting to round file disposition that for which continued retention serves no useful ongoing purpose.

As I indicated in a general memo following our community open house undertaking back in June, I was pleased with the orderliness and absence of clutter which was exposed to the eyes of our guests on that occasion. Our guests on that day had to have been impressed, and I hope we can impress our trade guests equally.

Visitors invariably compliment us on our facilities and working environment, in large part because our equipment is modern and well maintained. While I recognize that a certain measure of clutter is normally unavoidable as we pursue our daily tasks, when we can treat guests to orderliness in and around our individual work areas, they are certainly going to extend us even higher marks as they relate their experiences to friends and associates.

And, just as a reminder, on Tuesday, October 13, many employee spouses will be visiting the building as well, to attend our special 40th anniversary ESOP meeting sessions, so we want to be mindful of that exposure as well.

Thanks for doing your part to make our company shine for its 40th anniversary celebrations.

From the head of a publishing house, the inspiration ... (turn the page)

October 1

To: All Employees

From: Lawrence

SUBJECT: POLICING WORK AREAS FOR UPCOMING
            TRADE OPEN HOUSE

Please tidy up your work areas for the October 12th Open
House.

Thank You

*... and from the employees,
the rewrite.*

-3-

Getting

- - - - - - - - - -

Personnel

- - - - - - - - - - - - -

My dad used to say "you can pick your friends but you can't pick your family," which, at the time, I was too young to take personally. To that folk saw you might add "nor the people you work for, alongside, or in spite of," although it makes for a cumbersome saying. First comes school, where, by the sheer accident of having a name that falls alphabetically behind yours, Dean Himmelreich lands behind you in every class right through college with unlimited access to your person granted by virtue of the gap between the seat and the desk back.

Next comes the workplace, where who knows what cubicle will abut yours and what it will hold? These are adults—for every shoe through the seat of grade school, there are dozens of ways they can end-run your initiatives, blunt your prerogatives, and unravel the knit of your career with the only redress being whatever pithy non sequitur you can summon up at the Christmas party, where, it is to be hoped, everybody drinks heavily so there are no reliable witnesses. It's no accident self-employment has been rising steadily for decades; it can only be a matter of time before no one works for anyone else, as opposed to the current system where it only works out that way.

Managing all this can seem an insurmountable task. There are, after all, many more people than there are people skills, and many of the hardiest strains have deflected accountability (or even, for God's sake, a suggestion) for so long they are like bacteria antibiotics can't touch. They're not even personnel any more; they're "Human Resources," which naturally makes you wonder if strip mining, clear cutting, or damming are now in order (may one speak of human resources being "harvested"?).

Japanese management techniques, briefly thought to be the work motivation panacea, panned out when nobody sang the office song or wanted to hold the receptionist's ankles while she did sit ups. Some of the thought has been utilized in the process of Total Quality Management, although there are days you have to wonder whether your *Kanban* really raises your *Kaizen*, or if, in fact, your *Dantotsu* has gotten about as good as it's going to get. And the Baldrige Quality Award? Please, the man died falling off a horse!

When all the workshops have done their empowering, all the facilitators have dropped their paradigms and run, when all the total quality has been "Deming'd" to within an inch of its baseline, you still end up with people: you can't shear 'em, you can't milk 'em, and while they may talk the talk, and even walk the walk, they may never "understand the severity of what [they] are about to endure."

SUBJECT:　Work Schedules

The official business hours of the District Office including POD's are 8:00 a.m. to 4:30 p.m. This means that <u>all</u> personnel have schedules that provide for a continuous 8 hour work day with an officially recognized half hour lunch period. The work schedule must be the same for each day of the week. Variable daily schedules are not permissible.

An employee <u>MUST</u> contact his/her supervisor as soon as possible, but not later than two hours after the scheduled starting time on any day that he/she will not arrive by the scheduled starting time. If for any reason the supervisor is not available, then the employee must talk with the next higher level of authority. Contacting other personnel within the division or office does not satisfy this requirement. All supervisors must contact the District Director and in his absence must talk with the person designated to act in the Director's behalf.

All employees are entitled to take a 15 minute break in the morning and a 15 minute break in the afternoon. Personnel electing to take breaks must use the break or lose it. Furthermore, employees taking breaks are entitled to either 30 or 45 minutes for lunch dependent upon whether or not the employee chooses to take both breaks. An employee cannot elect to forego a break or a lunch period in order to leave work early or report to work at a later time. All lunch periods will begin no earlier than 11:00 a.m. and must be completed by 2:00 p.m. Each supervisor must assure during district office business hours that an adequate number of division staff are present to respond to telephone calls and other inquiries/requests.

(continues)

Each supervisor must approve and have on file in the division, with a copy to Administration, a schedule for all personnel under their supervision indicating lunch and break periods. The establishment of a scheduled time for breaks and lunch does not prohibit flexibility depending upon the needs of the division and the individual employee on any given day as determined/concurred with by the Supervisor. However, the length of time allowed is not flexible and the option selected can not be variable - an employee must maintain the option selected. The option can be changed by completing a new "employee work schedule" approved by the Supervisor.

Yeah, but do we hafta?

OFFICE MEMO

Subject: | Coffee water test

Time: | 2:00 PM

Date: | 9/4/91

A REPORT ON THE COFFEE WATER TEST

Bottom line: The best estimate, on current data corrected by guesswork, is that the cost of using bottled water for all our coffee would increase the cost of a cup by more than one cent but less than two cents.

Background: You may remember that, having raised the possibility of using bottled water for our coffee, I was tasked with investigating the costs and benefits of my suggestion. The empiricism I employed yielded anomolous findings: on their face, the results showed that the average size of a coffee cup in the division is 30 oz. Recognizing the appropriate relationship between discretion and valor in the reporting of paradigm-shattering data, I asked Paul for help. Between us, we established the following prospective study, which should help us to arrive at a good decision.

Method: Paul and I will contribute 5 gallons of bottled water to the study. We will do this by posting prominent signs on the coffee machine and water cooler, asking everyone to use the bottled water and to make a check mark on the form provided. When we have used up the five gallons, the study will be over. There are two sorts of variables: subjective and objective. The

(continues)

subjective variables are 1) whether you can taste an improvement and 2) whether the convenience of avoiding trips to the bathroom is large enough to bear the likely additional cost, given whatever the experience with taste enhancement turns out to be. We feel no need to be rigorous about taste enhancement testing methods: if it isn't obviously better, then that's an important datum. The objective variable is how many pots and cups the five gallons will create. One might have thought that the cup to pot ratio would have been the easiest part of the first set of calculations. But not so: there is an apparent discrepancy between estimated pots made per three-month period and cups marked drunk in the same period. Hence the need for a prospective study.

Paul and I will appreciate receiving your comments on the taste and convenience questions.

This is coffee, mind you. Beyond that it can only get more complicated...

April 17

To: All Employees

From: Sean

Tomorrow we will begin the remodeling program for our office.

It will have some structural changes around the reception area, operations area and near Julie's desk. It will be carpeted, painted, wallcovered and generally made neat and new.

None of this effort will be of any value if we return to our old ways. Piling up old research, charts, statements or anything else on the floor is forever more verboten.

There is a close kinship between people who tape things to the walls of their offices and people who put cars on blocks in their front yards. NO MORE! If it isn't framed, don't put it on your wall. If you have things that you would like to occasionally refer back to, I will be glad to supply you with a clipboard. Consider the appearance you present to your visitors. Would you tape stuff to your living room wall? Enough said.

Get ready. Anything on the floor will be pitched. Anything taped to walls will be thrown out. Painting will begin Thursday.

What do you say we tape "Sean" to the wall?

PERSONNEL DOCKING SLIP

Joyce
_____

Your paycheck on ___*5/17*___ will be docked
___*.05 if a*___ hours as you were ~~leave~~ *late 3 min.* without pay
on ___*5/1*___.

You are not permitted to use vacation or compensatory time
to cover this as both must be prior authorized.

Debbie
_____
Personnel/Payroll Department

Gotcha!

September 20

Dear Ms. DeLuca

Enclosed is a copy of the contract which we mishandled greatly
and for which we offer our apologies. There was no excuse
except to relate to what happened as follows.

On Thursday, September 14th., we sent our tractor-trailer with
two experienced men and $850 in cash to Chicago via
Cleveland. They completed work on a tent outside Cleveland at
4:30 p.m. Saturday, and left for Chicago. At 11:00 p.m., they
arrived in Indiana and ate supper at a Truckstop, which we
have verified. At this point the foreman was to go to a motel
and be at the Restaurant the next morning at 8:00 O'clock.

(The following was related by the Assistant Foreman on his
return to Memphis).

After supper at the Truckstop the foreman (without any
company authorization) drove to Milwaukee to visit relatives.
The assistant went to his own relatives and the next morning
could not locate the foreman, nor did he have the keys to the
tractor.

At approximately noon Sunday, your company contacted our
Operations' Manager, He was at a complete loss since we
knew the men should have been in the area Saturday. He
contacted local relatives and was told by the Asst. Foreman's
Mother, that her son called at 9 O'clock Sunday and said they
were outside Chicago and on the way to the city. When they
were not there by 2:00 p.m., he called the company which
handles our vehicles nationwide to see if they had a mechanical
break-down. They reported no calls.

At this point the Operations Manager called me and I contacted
another tent company. They had a crew working Sunday and

(continues)

would send two experienced men out at 4:00 p.m. They gave each man $300 expense money and instructed them to call immediately on arrival in Chicago.

The men never arrived and the General Manager of the tent company talked to the Police about an all points bulletin to see if anything happened.

At 3:00 a.m., with two crews disappearing and at after least ten (10) phone calls, the Operation's Manager left by car for Chicago. He arrived about 8:00 a.m., and the tent was removed.

Subsequently, we learned that the foreman returned the tractor-trailer to Indiana late Sunday night and abandoned it. Monday the assistant called to relate his story and we immediately sent him by taxi to the Restaurant to help the Manager. We also found out that one of the men spent his $300 when they arrived in Chicago on an illegal purpose and arrived about noon at the

All of these men have been terminated.

The makings of a picaresque novel- something like 'Tom Jones' of tents. For the film I see Liam Neeson and Danny De Vito as the crew, Olympia Dukakis as the mother.

Memo/Q travel procedures

There has been some questions about our Q system I hope this will help answer some of them. The supervisor or lead agent will be the designated Q person. The Q person will add A received line in the 5N cross remarks when working on the reservation. Q will display the record locator add the Q received line then end the PNR, pull the reservation up by record locator and work on record out of queue. This will let the agent know the reservation has been received by Q and is being worked on and not to add or change anything on the PNR at this time. This should eliminate us from giving each other simos. The Q person will complete the reservation according to what is documented in your 5N cross remarks. Thats just one more reason why your remarks should be clear and accurate, document, document, document. The Q person will issue all tickets that need to be ticketed and set up for delivery or airborned. Q will phase reservations for negociated fares if needed for immediately ticketing. Q will issue prepays if the central prepaid desk is closed. The agents will still be responsible for monitoring the reservations to make sure this is done. Agents will be responsible for any follow ups needed, or to contact passenger due to any discrepancies on there reservation. When Q is completed with the reservation He/She will add a completed line in 5N cross remarks, 5N/19oct/S0/Q completed.qued. This will document that the Q person has completed the reservation and any remark errors or accounting errors the booking agent will not be cited for A error by our designated QC person, which usually means our wonderful and appreciated. If you have a rush PTA or ticket please let our Q person know right away, dont wait A hour then advise them. The Q person will also queue the completed reservation to all the appropriate queues and field offices. If you have any questions or ideas to help make our department run more efficiently and improving our phone report please drop A note in my folder.

Lets make our 85 percent goal, 1 know we can.
Thanks

Ever wonder why your travel agent has that look on her face while she's checking availability?

To: Accounting   From: Human Resources

The following is what occurred concerning the 7 hrs of CC (unpaid leave) entered on Christy's timecard for 8-18.

Beginning on Wednesday 8-26 Data Entry (CRT's) entered into a slack work period in which CC was offered for 7 consecutive work days. The CC entered under 8-18 was actually taken on Friday, July 28th, but because nightshift timecards are submitted on Thursday nites (in this case, July 27th) Friday nite entries are carried over to the following week's time-cards. (The only exception to this procedure occurs when on Friday nites an operator is gone for the entire 8 hours. In this situation the supervisor may OK a change to a timecard before the van leaves with the timecards. Any absence or CC etc. which is for less than this 8 hours cannot be accounted for til the following week!) Therefore, in getting back to the 8-18 entry for Christy, because it was too late to account for the 7 hours of CC on July 28th this time was carried over to the week of July 31st. However, during this 4 day week Christy took CC every nite of the week (each night for at least 3 hours) so that any attempt to enter the 7 hrs from July 28th would exceed 8 hours of CC (which is not acceptable). This then carried the 7 hours of CC over to the week of Aug. 7. Christy was on vacation for the entire week which carried the 7 hours of CC over to the week of August 14. Christy then put the 7 hours of CC on Friday because it had been a Friday (July 28th) when she actually took company convenience.

Carry-over time from a Friday nite to the following week is common practice on nightshift timecards because they are OK'd and submitted every Thursday nite. A possible solution to eliminating this carryover is to hold nightshift timecards til Saturday or Monday and mail them at that time. Or possibly the department secretary could call in the Friday nite entries early Monday AM. You do run the risk of having to account for numerous changes by phone some Mondays under this second solution.

You've heard of the famous "CC Rider"? This one is "Company Convenience," or unpaid leave that is treated as an excused absence.

INBOX 51

Jan 18 at 19:31 EST

bulletin: SECURITY BULLETIN

from: Services

subject: Demo Software Recall

*** SECURITY BULLETIN ***

It has been reported that a modification has
been made to the desktop file on some of the
demo software diskettes for the computer. The
icon for the application has been changed to
show a sexually explicit picture when the demo
is started. This demo software has found its way
into our customers; in one case, at very high
levels. Security is asking that employees
retrieve and hold all copies of this demo until
an investigation on this matter has been
completed. DO NOT provide customers with ANY
copies of this software until further notice.

Security Services
Manager, Information Security
End of INBOX 51

*"...found its way into our customers"?
Man, that's software!*

TO: Abby

FROM: Judy

SUBJECT: Weekly Schedules

DATE: February 25

Please note that since you are not my supervisor, it is not your responsibility to request a business staff member remind me to turn in my schedule to the front desk. The purpose of schedules is two-fold:

1. So that the receptionist knows whether a staff member is in or out of the office for the purpose of referring telephone calls

2. So that the employee's supervisor knows the weekly schedule of their employee and can modify schedules if necessary based on schedules of other employees.

Since none of these apply in your case, your behavior in asking Joan to ask me for my schedule was completely out-of-line. Be advised that it is not necessary for you to know the working schedule of every executive staff member. For this reason, you are not permitted behind the counter to review schedules. I have also directed that executive staff schedules be kept in a different location to avoid such "snooping". If you need to know a staff member's availability, you may inquire with the receptionist the next available time they are in the office.

There are a lot of people impersonating supervisors out there. It is well to drive stakes through their hearts whenever possible.

MEMO

To: Murray

From: Vincent

Date: August 4

Re: Job Safety

I think that you should be made aware of a very dangerous condition which exists here. I was recently blueprinting. As I reached over to align a print, my tie became caught in the infeed rollers and I began to be drawn toward almost certain injury. Fortunately, the very slow speed at which we now print allowed me to think and plan a self-rescue. I received no injury and now live to tell of this experience.

I recommend that the office policy of requiring ties be re-evaluated given the facts of my harrowing experience.

It's easy to blame ties, but it's not hard to imagine your dickey getting caught in there, either.

TELECONFERENCE REPORT

To: Team A   Conference Date: 26 February
From: John Jamison

This report is intended to summarize the results of the weekly teleconference. The following people were on the call:

Customer	GD	MDC	NAA
		John Jamison	

Discussion/Agreements

Jamison made the observation that their seemed to be less interest lately in the Telecons. The rest of the callers were polled, and Jamison agreed with himself. A detailed discussion then ensued, and it was decided that four possibilities existed:

(1) everyone else is too busy,
(2) everyone else lost the phone number,
(3) everyone else forgot the telecon time and day of the week, or
(4) Jamison dialed the wrong number, at the wrong time, on the wrong day.

Since it is unlikely that all six of the other usual participants could have simultaneously been too busy, lost the number, or forgotten the time and day, it was concluded that Jamison must be in error. It was decided that someone should verify the telecon phone number, time, and day. In addition, it was decided that a telecon once a week might be excessive at this time. After much discussion Jamison finally agreed to take the action item.

Action Items

Jamison-Verify the telecon phone number, time of day, and day of the week. Schedule the next few telecons for every other week until further notice

Action Item Resolution

The telecon is scheduled for Tuesdays at 11:00 AM.

Jamison leaps on the grenade.

inter-office communication

to: Oscar Roland   **date:** Sept. 16

from: Norman Eastwood

subject: DEMAND FOR SATISFACTION

Please be informed that your erroneous confrontation with me regarding the opening of bids not only maligned my character, but caused me the utmost of humiliation in the presence of my peers.

Since you were, as I so politely tried to point out to you in the first place, **WRONG**, I feel called upon to demand satisfaction either through a public apology in the presence of said peers, or a duel at first light, with weapons of your choice.

Your faithful servant.

Chivalry is not dead.

Safety Newsletter

DATE 1/19   NEWSLETTER NO. 654   DISTRIBUTION ALL EMPLOYEES

WARNING:

BINDER CLIP FAILURE

An employee recently attempted to place a binder clip (Stores Item26-755.00) on several sheets of paper and the clip broke in the flexing area of the clamp. The individual was not injured, but the break left two sharp edges that could have caused a laceration. There was no evidence of misuse that would have caused the break. This is the first reported failure of this type on the plant.

Although the above incident appears to be an isolated case, these devices should be used with caution. The clamp portion is fabricated of spring steel and any breakage will probably be sudden and without prior indication that failure is imminent. Clips should be opened with steady thumb and forefinger pressure; never wider than the design capacity, (3/8 inch, in this case). Clips should not be used as "finger exercisers". Prolonged, repeated opening will cause metal fatigue in the flexing area.

TAKE HEED!!

Exclusive! Major safety concern at a nuclear power plant!

INTER-OFFICE MEMORANDUM

TO: Mitch   Date:

FROM: Andrea

SUBJECT: Door buzzard

As you know, even though it is very difficult for me to open the door promptly because of the buzzard being in an inconvenient place (i.e. on the wall and beyond my arm length) I have made a valiant effort to open the door for everyone. And most of the time, each person already has their door key in the door, but I still try let them in even when I'm away from the front desk and next to the terminal.

I bring this attention to you because it's been over a year since our discussion about moving the buzzard to a more convenient place and even though you have done <u>nothing</u> about this problem, I have made sure to let everyone in when I'm in front or near my desk. However, I overheard complaints about how I'm letting go of the buzzard too soon. At all the times I have tried to buzz people in, even though they already have a key in the door. Besides that, because of my back problems, I do not lean over while I'm sitting down like I use to. As you may or may have not noticed, I now stand up and buzz people in. As it is, I'm having trouble leaning forward as I'm standing up and still hold the buzzard at the same time as I sometimes lose my balance. You may have been aware of this when I tried to let you in and my fingers slipped from the buzzard.

Since I'm still having problems with the door and now I'm hearing complaints, I would like to know what your intentions are in solving this dilemma. I would appreciate your getting back to me promptly on this matter.

P.S.: Please resolve this before review time.

Fuzzy logic computer chips are all well and good, but the fuzzy individual will never be replaced.

To: All Employees

We have been having a lot of problems with people taking food and drink that does not belong to them. In the future, if someone takes something that belongs to someone else (personal or company items), you will be charged through a payroll deduction $5.00 over the value of the item. If it happens a second time, you will be terminated. We will not tolerate steeling from the company or from a fellow employee!

Also, I would like to mention that everyone enjoys a donut. The company is kind enough to provide them once a week and the employees are kind enough to provide them on Saturday mornings. Please share. Each employee is to eat "one" donut at their designated break time! If there are any left over, you are welcome to another "one" at lunch time.

I hope that I have made myself clear. Do unto others as you would have them do unto you.

The Golden Rule: Terminate others as you would have them terminate you.

TO: All Department Directors
FROM: Director, Food & Nutrition Services
DATE: December 10
SUBJECT: Annual Coffee Allowance

Please complete the following flowchart to determine if your department is eligible for a coffee allowance again this year. This allowance is intended to ensure that employees do not have to subsidize courtesy coffee needs within their departments.

Department has a coffee pot

YES

Only staff consume coffee from this pot

STOP
You are not eligible for coffee allowance

Only visitors/patients consume coffee from this pot

No need for coffee allowance. You should be ordering coffee on an Inter-departmental Requisition from Food & Nutrition.

Complete the information in Box 1

Both staff and visitors/patients consume coffee from this pot

You are eligible for a coffee allowance

Complete the information in Box 1 and 2

a coffee flow chart?

NO

STOP
You are not eligible for coffee allowance

- -

BOX 1
Name _____   Dept. _____

Dept. Account No. _____

BOX 2
Ave. monthly consumption by visitors/patients _____ cups/mo.

Ave. monthly consumption by staff   _____ cups/mo.

Please return this form to _____ by Friday, Dec. 20, in order to receive your allowance.

November 12

Memorandum

To: Division Chiefs, All Center Lunchroom Refrigerator Users

From: Superintendent

Subject: Refrigerator Contents - The Caper of the Frozen Bird and "Sail Weasel"

A number of us (the vocal majority that counts) believe it is entirely inappropriate, unnecessary, distasteful and perhaps even unsafe to store whole or remnants of animal, plant or insect unprocessed remains in the lunchroom refrigerator. In other words don't do it.

There is a new freezer with the price tag still on it available for such use at our other office.

The lunchroom refrigerator should serve as a place to store an employee's lunch, snacks and drinks. It's not the place for your week's grocery supply or cases of cold drinks.

If I may share a personal observation, I found something in the refrigerator that I thought was food — but it did appear to have considerable fur on it. Full analysis showed that at one time it was cheese.

If I may suggest, you each have a responsibility to help keep the refrigerator clean — the contents fresh — and the bulk down so all can use it.

With everyone's cooperation, it will work. Thanks.

From a national park in Wyoming, a new look at what lingers in the back of the refrigerator.

Date: January 18

To: Audit Unit Members, Dept of Transportation

From: Supervisor

Subject: POPCORN SURVEY

A request by staff members in various units of Room 151 has been forwarded requesting approval to pop popcorn in Room 151. Although the end result may not be strictly by "majority rule", Gary has asked that the supervisors conduct a survey of the opinion of the staff regarding this matter, and ask that we gather your comments/reasons. If you wish to express a view on the subject, please complete the following and return to me at your earliest convenience.

1. Do microwave food smells <u>other than popcorn</u> bother you in Room 151?
   Yes   No   Undecided   No comment

2. Do you think the food smells <u>other than popcorn</u> portray an undesirable image to counter customers?
   Yes   No   Undecided   No comment

3. Do microwave food smells from <u>popcorn</u> bother you in Room 151?
   Yes   No   Undecided   No comment

4. Do you think the food smells from <u>popcorn</u> portray an undesirable image to counter customers?
   Yes   No   Undecided   No comment

5. Does the smell of popcorn popped in a microwave in another room, but opened in Room 151 bother you?
   Yes   No   Undecided   No comment

(continues)

6. Do you think the smell of popcorn popped in a microwave in another room, but opened in Room 151 portrays an undesirable image to counter customers?

Yes   No   Undecided   No comment

7. Do you favor allowing popcorn to be popped in the microwave in Room 151?

Yes   No   Undecided   No comment

8. Comments:

_____

_____

_____

_____

_____

Signature (optional) _____

Boy, they're busy at transportation, and...

INTER-OFFICE memo

TO: DISTRIBUTION

SUBJECT: Popcorn Test

DATE: June 22

FROM: DATA PROCESSING

The results from the popcorn test yesterday follows:

  Bags numbers 1 - 20 — Jane's Burger Hut
  Bags numbers 21 - 41 — Billy's Drivein

Of the 33 results that were returned:

  11 people prefer Billy's
  22 people prefer Jane's

Of those 16 who ate Jane's:

  10 thought it was Billy's
   6 thought it was Jane's

Of those 17 who ate Billy's:

  12 thought it was Billy's
   5 thought it was Jane's

So what does this tell us? Most people say they prefer Jane's, but don't know they're eating it!!

            THANKS!

...in data processing.

DRESS CODE PROCEDURES

I. ADHERENCE TO PROPER DRESS AND APPAREL:

All employees shall act as role models for clients by adhering to the dress code rules. Each employee shall display proper dress and apparel in an adult, mature manner conforming to social/or moral standards of decency.

II. SPECIFIC DRESS CODE GUIDELINES:

1) trousers or jeans are preferred, however, shorts and skirts may be worn if the hemline is no higher than the employee's handwidth above the knee. To determine this, the Supervisor will ask the employee to measure a hands width above the knee and proceed accordingly.

2) no obscene T-shirts

3) no halter tops/cut off blue jeans/biker pants

4) clean and neat in appearance

III. PROCESS:

All employees in a supervisory or management position will be responsible for enforcing the requirements set forth in the policy. Employees who fail to comply with the policy shall be directed to clock out their supervisor and advised to change clothing and return to work in compliance with the policy. Time off from work for such purposes shall be deducted from the employee's pay. At the time of the first incident, the employee will be verbally counseled by the supervisor. Each additional incident will be administratively reviewed for possible disciplinary action. The guidelines for progressive discipline will be followed in this regard.

(continues)

If an employee disagrees with the supervisor concerning his/her noncompliance with this policy, they have the right to appeal the pay lost to the STAFF APPEARANCE COMMITTEE. The employee must decide to appeal at the time he/she is being directed to punch out and notify the supervisor, or no appeal is permitted. At the time the employee is directed to clock out they are to sign a form which states that they are or are not going to appeal this decision. If the employee appeals the decision, prior to being sent home, the employee will be photographed by the GDC police and the matter referred to the SAC. The employee may choose not to be photographed, but still appeal to the committee with the Supervisor and Union Representative who witnessed the employee's dress.

Patent leather shoes should be worn at your own discretion.

TO: Staff

FROM: Steve Kichick

SUBJECT: Corporate Citizenship (Part 85)

When 33 professionals work in close proximity for extended periods of time, it is to be expected that certain frictions will arise. Occasionally, however, those frictions become unbearable and it becomes my duty to attempt to smooth over the rough spots. In particular, I would like to elicit your support in the following areas:

1. Although we have all been advised of the need to conserve water and may have even implemented rigorous water-conservation measures at our own homes, in the workplace it is always advisable to flush.

2. It is not reasonable to expect that the "cup fairy" will wash your filthy coffee cup simply because you have placed it in the sink. If you have reached your current age without learning the fine art of washing dishes, let me know and I will arrange for a tutorial at my house.

3. The "cup fairy" does not moonlight as the "coffee fairy." Making a new pot of coffee (or a new pot of water) does not require much effort. By my calculations, a pot of coffee holds about eight cups. If you drink four cups a day, you should, on average, make a pot every two days. (Those of you with advanced quantitative skills may want to check my math.) If you drink coffee and are not <u>regularly</u> making coffee, you are shirking your duties.

4. The chief has indicated that he wishes to have the lights, which illuminate our display cases at the ends of the fourth floor, turned on during working hours. Those who follow him down the hall and turn off those lights as soon

(continues)

as he has turned them on have made your point, but the savings in electricity is more than offset by the wear and tear on the switch and the general increase in office tension (borne primarily by me).

Thank you for your attention to these nettlesome matters. If your co-workers annoy you in other ways, please feel free to bring it to my attention. If I annoy you, keep it to yourself.

What isn't clear is why 33 professionals, working in close proximity for extended periods of time, would stop flushing. Perhaps the literature on naked mole rats would be illuminating (like the display cases?)

ACCESS TO SMOKING STAFF ROOM (105) ON SATURDAYS

1. Go to entrance to Reference and Government Services Division (2nd floor-Room 206 by elevator 2 (yellow). Use key (short) to unlock and then lock the door back and close.

2. If light switch (located to the right is not on) turn on and leave on.

3. Go through Reference and Government Services Division to door leading to the Great Hall. You can leave through this door without using a key.

4. Either take the elevator or stairs to the first (1st) floor and then proceed to Room 105.

5. To return to your work area, either take stairs or elevator to the second floor.

6. Enter door to Reference and Government Services Division from Great Hall. Use of key (long) is required.

7. Proceed through Reference and Government Services Division to Door B2-6 by Elevator 2. No key required to enter elevator lobby area. Make sure that door is closed and locked.

8. One set of keys is provided to the Genealogy Section and one to the Smith Library for those who need access to Smoking Staff Room on Saturday.

9. Insuring security of the building by locking doors is required in order to continue to have access on Saturdays to the Smoking Staff Room. Your cooperation is required and appreciated.

Several people have quit along the way.

-4-

What You
- - - - - - - - - - - -
Can Do
- - - - - - - - - -
for Your Country
- -

L et's face it, everybody's received Christmas cards from 1953 42 years later with 31¢ postage due—but the fact is they were in remarkably good condition (nestled, as it were, between the sorter and the wall in PO substation number 114 and thus not subject to the ravages of time other correspondence must endure), arriving only slightly yellowed and with the added sentiment of finding that one or the other or both correspondents have passed on. It's too easy to jump from these tales (which make excellent holiday newspaper filler, after all) to conclude that the fault lies not in the stars but in government service.

After all, looking just at the postal service, most of us get most of our mail in mostly readable condition most of the time; and while that's not the official motto, it's still a pretty good record in this day and age. Besides, how many of us without natural fur have to work outside in climates ranging from cyclonic to permafrost or must portage pools of brackish water trailed by hell hound terriers all in the quest of delivering Procter and Gamble's latest tampon sample to an elderly single male? Government workers, that's who. Walk a mile in your carrier's frozen Redwings and you'll soon forgive the occasional pile of first-class mail burning in an underpass in Chicago. It's a stress thing.

So it is, too, for the civil servants everywhere charged with the daunting task of running our states' and nation's agencies under a barrage of guidelines, policies, and legislative fiats. No one likes to be categorized, yet here you have GS 11's prevented by statute from mingling with GS 7's, pigeonholed by ratings as workers, soldiers, burrowers, egg handlers, leaf masticators, and lookouts, all for the benefit of a Queen they never see.

And what thanks do they get? These memos.

The following rules govern parking in our employee parking lots:

1. The parking lot is to be used only by employees and only while on official duty. If a non-employee rides to work with an employee, they must be dropped off prior to entering our lot.

2. All vehicles must be parked "head-in".

3. Only managers level 17 and above are allowed to park in the lot behind the K-Dock. Supervisors are allowed to park in the fenced first two rows on the west end of the main lot. All other employees will park in the main lot.

4. When two people in the same household work for the Service, and one is a supervisor and one is a craft employee, the following applies:

A. The vehicle may have both a blue (supervisor) sticker and a white (employee) sticker. This will allow the vehicle to be parked in the blue lot when driven by a supervisor, and parked in the white lot when driven by a craft employee.

B. When a craft employee and a supervisor drive together, the craft employee must be dropped off <u>prior</u> to parking in the blue (supervisor) lot. If the vehicle has both a blue and white sticker, both employees may drive together and park in the white lot.

Generally speaking, blues and whites should not mate as it makes parking all but impossible.

DEPARTMENT OF THE ARMY
UNITED STATES ARMY RESERVE TRAINING CENTER

MEMORANDUM FOR SEE DISTRIBUTION   28 OCTOBER

SUBJECT: Opening Windows

1. We experience several problems when windows are opened. I have recently gone through the entire facility and locked all windows for some specific reasons. We encourage and request that people do not open windows.

2. First. The windows in the seven story leased building are double sided windows. One side is treated with a special "Gold" coating which reflects the sun rays and heat. The other side is normal safety glass. The gold side must be on the outside and the normal glass to the inside. It is easy to identify from a distance when windows are improperly closed. Most important to remember is that when the normal side is out facing the sun, that surface absorbs the heat which may cause the window to explode if over heating occurs. In addition, when windows are not properly closed it presents a checker board appearance on the Fred's building which our lessor has taken issue. If you open a window please make sure it is closed with the "Gold" side out.

3. Second. People have opened windows and not completely closed them which has resulted in rain entering and damaging the facility. Please leave the windows closed and locked. Please, if you open a window make sure it is properly closed and locked.

4. Third. During a recent drill some windows were opened and wasps flew into the offices and building. The issue with wasps or insect nests on the building has been addressed with the lessor. By nature of the design of the seven story building, typically during this season wasps continually build nests next

(continues)

the windows to seek warmth. Removal is possible but a continuing process. The topic of insect infestation will be addressed to the lessor as a separate issue.

5. Fourth. Opening the windows creates an imbalance in the heating, ventilation, and air-conditioning system (HVAC). The imbalance effects the temperature in the entire building.

SUBJECT:

Opening Windows

6. The seven story building has a heating, ventilation, and air-condition system which is designed to provide quality temperature control through the entire building. Accordingly, it should not be necessary to open windows. Acknowledge, in the past we have experienced some problems with the system which were promptly responded to by the lessor.

7. Please disseminate this information to all your unit personnel. Above and beyond all, it is a safety issue.

From the Department of the Army. Another problem with windows; closing them behind you on the way out.

Tues 4-Sep 12:39 EDT Sys 150

Subject: DEGRADATION OF NOMEX FLIGHT SUITS

PASS TO: STATE ADJUTANT GENERAL

Further tests conducted at the laboratories reveal that methane gas has an accumulative effect on Nomex material and is directly proportional to the moisture content of the gas. therefore para 3-23 is changed as follows: "if the Nomex has been subjected to 100 or more exposures to gastro-intestinal vapor attacks that the Nomex must be subjected to a stress test. this test consists of firmly grasping the seat of the pants with both hands and vigorously tugging. if the seam or material stays intact the Nomex is serviceable. repeat this procedure with every 50 attacks."

The procedure is invalid if any gastro-intestinal vapor attack feels wet to the touch.

Forscom msg Aug 90 is quoted in it's entirety for clarification:

A. Recent tests conducted at the laboratories reveal that methane gas degrades the fire retardant properties of Nomex. To prevent abnormal wear of Nomex and unnecessary risk to crewmembers, para 3-23, is changed as follows: "no one wearing Nomex is authorized to relieve themselves of gastro-intestinal vaporous accumulations without first removing their Nomex flight suits to that portion of the legs below the knees."

B. This change should not be construed to allow crewmembers to arbitrarily "moon" innocent passers-by. the utmost discretion must be used by all crewmembers.

From the Air Force, a memo on flying by the seat of your pants.

Inter-Office Correspondence

Date: November 2

To: All City Managers

From: Commissioner

As many, if not all, of you are aware, there have been a few public agencies that have been embarrassed lately due to the lack of control of the employees they are responsible for. Personally, I always try to make a habit of taking nothing for granted. When I see reports of employee abuses, as I have lately, it serves as a reminder to me that we all have a responsibility to be up on what our employees are doing on city time.

As an individual in a responsible management position, it is incumbent upon you to be aware of the actions of employees under your direction. I strongly suggest you allot some time to assess just how aware you are of what is happening within your operation and assure yourself that your management controls are in place and working. This is no time to leave your guard down.

We cannot be everywhere and see everything, but there is no excuse for some of the gross abuses that have been exposed lately. I am trusting you will consider my comments and take them to heart.

From a large metropolis on the shores of Lake Erie, a sense of malaise.

November 4

Dear Education Program Administrator:

The United States Department of Agriculture (USDA) has asked this office to issue the following policy regulating the use of taco chips in reimbursable meals in our schools.

The USDA <u>prohibits</u> snack type foods, such as chips, to be used as a bread alternate for reimbursable meals. If ''taco chips'' are listed on a menu and used as a bread alternate for a meal, reimbursement for meals is to be denied.

However, USDA will accept menu titles such as taco pieces, taco medallions, or taco shells. On menus and production forms it is important to specify taco pieces, taco shells, taco medallions, etc., and insure that the menu items meet the following conditions:

1) must contain whole-grain or enriched meal or flour as a primary ingredient;

2) must be served as an accompaniment to, or as a recognizable part of, the main dish; and

3) must be served in correct portion sizes (one serving must weigh a minimum of .7 ounces).

USDA is very firm on this policy. Therefore, it is essential that you do not use the word ''chip'' on menus or production forms.

Sincerely,
Assistant Superintendent

Taco molecules?

MEMORANDUM

TO: Assistant Commissioners, Division and
                    Bureau Directors
               Regional Medical Directors
               District Health Directors

FROM: Bureau of Central Services, Department of Health

IMPORTANT INFORMATION CONCERNING
ROLLERBALL PENS

This office has received a number of complaints concerning rollerball pens, the most frequent being that they will not write. We have found, in this office that about 90% of the pens that seem to be unusable can be used by following the simple procedure listed below.

If upon taking a new pen from the box, you find it will not write, hold it point down and shake vigorously several times. Then attempt to write a series of large loops on a piece of plain white paper.

In most cases this will cause the pen to write. Attempting to make the pen write by trying to write on cardboard will usually not work.

Also, these pens are not suited for use on carbon or NCR sets of more than a two page set. Sufficient pressure to make a legible copy usually results in pushing the ball up inside the pen.

At present, we may not obtain these pens from any other source. We are hoping that there will be an improvement in quality on future shipments of this item from the contract vendor.

In this historic commonwealth in the south, health care forms are sometimes returned marked with a series of large loops.

memorandum

DATE: July 24

REPLY TO
ATTN OF: Chief, Mapping Center

SUBJECT: Weapons and Explosives

TO: All Employees

It has come to my attention that some of you may not be aware of the Federal regulation concerning the bringing of weapons and/or explosives onto Federal property. As a reminder, the Code of Federal Regulations, 41 CFR 101.20.313, states that no person entering or while on Federal property shall carry or possess firearms, other dangerous or deadly weapons, explosives, or items intended to be used to fabricate an explosive or incendiary device, either openly or concealed, except for official purposes. This regulation applies to all employees regardless of the intent. Failure to comply could result in disciplinary action ranging from a letter of warning to dismissal.

Thank you for your understanding and cooperation in this matter.

It's the "except for official purposes" that reassures me.

December 19

Dear Producers,

Final payments for the crop year are enclosed.

You have received approximately 50% of your payments to date. The first payment consisted of 40% of the anticipated payment of $1.83 for deficiency plus the diversion payment on 2.5% of your wheat base. 50% of the 40% was paid in cash subject to Gramm-Rudman reduction of 4.3% and the other 50% of the 40% was paid in Commodity Certificates. The 2.5% of the wheat base (diversion) was paid in certificates at that time.

Later, another payment was made on 10% of the anticipated and was in Commodity Certificates.

The payments, based on the maxium payment of $1.98/Bu; $1.38 subject to limitation and $.60 not subject to limitation, are to be computed so that the final payment on wheat is 50% cash subject to Gramm-Rudman 4.3% reduction and 50% in Commodity Certificates. You will notice that the anticipated payment on wheat was $1.83/Bu; the final is $1.98/Bu, or an additional $.15/Bu.

The final payment on barley subject to limitation is $.65/Bu and on oats subject to limitation is $.37/Bu. The amount not subject to limitation will not be paid until July of next year on feed grains.

We have double checked your payments in the County ASCS office and believe they are correct. However, computers have "glitches" and humans make errors, so check for yourself.

Have a Merry Christmas and a Happy New Year.

Office Staff

A Christmas greeting forwarded from a farmer in Montana — when the USDA is making a list, it's worth checking it twice.

Date: April 11

To: CBT Program Managers

From: Program Coordinator, Competency Based
Testing Program
Bureau for Education Statistics and Testing

Subject: Team Motivation Workshops

Several weeks ago this Bureau sent you information on a
workshop for CBT program managers entitled "Team
Motivation."

These workshops have been canceled because we did not
meet the minimum enrollment needed to hold them.

I apologize for any inconvenience this may cause you.
Please feel free to call me if you would like to discuss your
program.

*From America's Dairyland where
"team motivation" means
following the one with the bell.*

TO: All Offices

FROM: State Senate Sergeant at Arms

RE: Dealing with Potentially Disruptive People

The Capitol is a very open and accessible building in the center of a large urban area. Occassionally staff in the building find themselves dealing with individuals who are confused or potentially disruptive. Most of these people are harmless and will leave when asked, politely but firmly, to do so. If, however, you have contact with a person who refuses to leave or someone who makes you feel threatened you can discreetly call security for assistance by using a code phrase. Dial 6-7700, identify yourself and your location and ask about "typewriter repair". The actual phrase is "your typewriter is ready to be picked up" but the dispatcher will respond to any query involving a typewriter. The dispatcher will ask if you are having a problem and you can simply reply "yes".

The dispatcher will verify your location and an officer will be sent immediately.

Please be sure that everyone in your office is familiar with this procedure.

Capitol Security also has a 1 hour training class on effective methods of dealing and coping with distraught and disturbed persons. Hopefully we will be able to work out a number of dates and times for the class and we urge you to participate.

If you have any questions please feel free to call me at 6-1801.

On the other hand, if you actually need typewriter repair you could be wrestled to the ground.

-5-

Washroom Politics

‑ ‑

The fact that Lyndon Johnson would sometimes grant interviews while seated on the toilet has alway struck me as a great example of democracy in action, as does the workplace washroom with its bank of four or six great equalizers and ceramic Wall of Democracy free (hopefully) from the prying eye of Big Brother. By far the most saved, cherished (too strong a word, but I'm trying to make a point), and forwarded memos routed my way are headed "washroom," subheads "behavior" and "facilities." Executives in their private privies would do well to wait a turn at the employee version every so often if just to read the writing on the grout (although I'd advise against dialing any of the numbers). Afterwards, I would also recommend not scrawling your own expletives in a memo, as yours will not be so anonymous and stand a good chance of ending up on a desk (mine) already up to here in commode commands with the waters still rising.

Many executives are understandably uncomfortable with toilet training their employees (perhaps a retreat on Total Quality Flushing would be in order?), and I can appreciate that after fishing jelly rolls out of what is, after all, not a serving bowl, one would be tempted to disseminate something like "Do Not Flush Anything Down These Toilets Other Than Human Waste," but I say let it go, lest it become your epitaph at Trans Consolidated Securities. (Universal symbols always work—what about a sign with a long john circled in red with a slash through it? Or is that too ambiguous for the men's room?)

Crucial to the successful manager is not getting bogged down in unresolvable debates, of which a classic is the seat up/seat down dilemma (and the primary reason OSHA recommends separate washroom facilities). Personally, I swear I've been told by women at various times in my life to both leave the seat up and to leave the seat down, until I just don't know which way to turn (and they complain about that too!). The things that go on in this sphere are important to people, as the violent stool-shifting controversy indicates, and the indelible memory I have of walking in on a top radio personality in a major market standing on top of a sink to hide a stash of paper towels above a water tank.

As to the privacy issues inherent in any public toilet, interested as I am in the human condition, I hope never to know which of my workmates subscribes to the "scrunched up, scrunched up with overwrap, pleated or wrapped-around" school of toilet paper use (although I think I know which one doesn't flush), and would run for an imaginary page should a fellow worker ever begin to confide how regularly they used personal cleansing tissues after a bowel movement.

But, hey, that's just me.

January 18

TO: The Dean

FROM: The Dean's Office Staff

RE: The Rest Rooms

We just wanted to let you know that though we
appreciate the new double-ply toilet tissue,
which is softer and more durable than the
previous brand, we all find difficulty using the
new dispensers. The paper keeps getting jammed,
and it is not at all easy to pull out, with the
result that a lot is wasted and left in shreds
on the floor. We realize that the dispensers are
new, but perhaps they could be recycled to
another location and some more efficient models
could be installed here.

Continuing education.

To: President

From: Office of Continuing Education, Enrollment Coordinator

December 17

I am writing to you because I'm not sure to whom this letter should be addressed, and thought you might be able to forward it to the appropriate person. But more importantly I think that you should be aware of the following potential health hazard.

About a month ago, new toilet paper dispensers were installed in most/all of the restrooms.

They are improperly designed and very difficult (and at times impossible) to get paper out of. There is a constant mess of scraps of toilet paper on the restroom floors.

Aside from the frustration and mess, a much more pressing matter is at hand. And the point of this letter. Because one must really work at getting at the paper — trying to feed it through the dispenser etc. etc., there is always hand work/manipulation involved. These dispensers, therefore are <u>extremely</u> unsanitary.

Don't get me wrong. I'm not a fussy individual. As a matter of fact, I've spent a bit of time in the less-developed world.

But this is America.

My understanding is that a memo or somesuch has been filed with someone somewhere. But this is not the kind of matter that can be dealt with on a when-we-can-get-to-it basis. This is a health matter and must be taken seriously. This problem needs to be fixed immediately.

Thank you very much for your time.

From a prestigious design school, some real-life design applications from someone who "spent a bit of time in the less-developed world." (Around here maybe?)

MEMORANDUM

TO: ALL FEMALE OFFICE EMPLOYEES

FROM: Irving Howard

SUBJECT: LADIES RESTROOM

DATE: JANUARY 20

Two times this week our toilets have been plugged up. Two times this week I've had the maintenance crew unplug the toilet and inform me of what they found. In one week several sanitary pads, tampons, a half roll of toilet paper, and jelly rolls, that's right JELLY ROLLS — FOOD; all were flushed down the toilet.

I am having new toilet paper holders installed which should eliminate that problem. However I have asked you before and am asking again, PLEASE DO NOT FLUSH ANYTHING DOWN THESE TOILETS OTHER THAN HUMAN WASTE.

The ladies of the 3rd floor are the joke of the building, and other tenants don't understand why such disgusting, unsanitary habits have to happen. Frankly, neither do I.

This memo was pulled up with the next catch.

CORRESPONDENCE/MEMORANDUM

Date: 3/29

To: All Male Staff

From: Matt

Subject: Toilet Seat

It has been explained to my satisfaction that there is a valid reason for returning the toilet seat to the sitting position after use.

Please take care to see that this is done.

I hope you were sitting down at the time.

Campus Communication

October 17

TO: Jeffrey Allen, Dean
                School of Arts & Sciences

FROM: Wendy Colton, Director
                Science Lab

RE: A recurring problem

For at least the past four years there has been a problem with constant leakage of the toilets in the LA second floor women's rest room. I have discussed this with maintenance several times, but the problem has never really been corrected. In addition to being unsightly and inconvenient, pools of water on the floor are unsanitary and could cause accidents, as well as spotting shoes and the hem of slacks.

I am concerned about the possible consequences of this problem, and would appreciate any assistance you can offer. Thank you for your consideration.

Bathroom reading, in installments . . .

Campus Communication

<u>M E M O R A N D U M</u>

October 24

TO: Secretary, Native American Studies
               Secretary, Career/Life Planning
               Coordinator, Women's Studies
               Lecturer of Science

FROM: Jeffrey Allen, Dean
               School of Arts and Sciences

It is my understanding that on occasion there is excess water on the floor in the women's restroom on the second floor causing inconvenience and potential hazard. If this problem recurs, please call the Physical Plant and send me a very short note noting the problem and the date and time you contacted Physical Plant personnel.

I regret the inconvenience.

More! ⟶

Campus Communication

DATE: October 29

TO: Native American Studies Coordinator

FROM: Director/Physical Plant

SUBJ: <u>LADIES ROOM - 2ND FLOOR LIBERAL ARTS</u>

When the call regarding the plugged stool was received by the Physical Plant, the plumber responded immediately. He found that the stool flushed properly and didn't follow up with anyone on what the problem could have been. It has since been learned that this is a sporadic problem, that the stool does flush sometimes and does not at other times. This situation will be corrected.

The stall marked "Out of Order" has a cracked stool, which we ordered as soon as the crack was discovered. It has a 2-3 week delivery date.

There are women's toilet rooms at the entrance to the Library on 2nd floor, at the base of the stairs going from 2nd to 1st floor and directly above the 2nd floor toilet room on 3rd floor. I would think with this selection, a woman would not have to stand in line. <u>If walking seems to be a problem,</u> consider the people on 2nd floor where there is neither a <u>men's nor women's toilet area.</u>

cs

cc: Dean, School of Arts & Sciences

More! →

Campus Communication

February 3

TO: Director, Physical Plant

FROM: Coordinator, Native American Studies

RE: Ladies Room - 2nd Floor Liberal Arts

Once again, the perennial problem of leakage in the rest room is becoming obvious. As of today at 9:45 a.m., the third stall had a puddle which was draining across the rest room floor. Aside from the annoyance, this can also present a health hazard which needs attention.

Is it possible to correct this problem permanently? Thank you for your assistance.

cc: Dean, School of Arts & Sciences

More! →

Campus Communication

DATE: February 7

TO: Coordinator, Native American Studies

FROM: Thomas Jensen, Director — Physical Plant

SUBJ: <u>LADIES ROOM 2ND FLOOR L.A. —</u>
          <u>WATER ON FLOOR</u>

Thank you for your memo bringing to our attention this water problem. We would prefer that when you have an immediate problem that indicates a water leak, you call the Physical Plant office immediately rather than putting a memo through the campus mail. The memo you wrote on February 3 was not received in our office until February 5 in the p.m. We had our plumber work on the problem February 6. Had you called this problem to our attention on the 3rd, we could have immediately had the problem fixed.

The cause of this water leak was not readily apparent. In fact, by just flushing the stool, our shop personnel could find no leaking water at all. This is probably why our custodians did not report the problem. One of our shop persons had to actually sit on the stool and shift weight fairly violently while the stool was being flushed in order to cause the problem to occur. It was discovered that a seal was not holding properly when there was a fairly active shifting of weight on the stool.

It is impossible to anticipate this type of problem and to make any modifications that would permanently solve the problem. The main cause of malfunctions in this area is the extremely heavy use this restroom receives.

cc: Math Lab
Dean - Arts & Sciences

More!

Campus Communication

February 11

TO: Thomas Jensen, Director, Physical Plant

FROM: Jeffrey Allen, Dean, School of Arts and
            Sciences

RE: VIOLENT SHIFTING STOOL SITTERS —
            LADIES ROOM, SECOND FLOOR, LA
            BUILDING

I have reviewed your memorandum with Wendy Colton
who advises me that she is reasonably certain that there
are no violent stool shifters. However, because of your
communication, I am asking her to continue to interview
and ascertain the name of the party or parties who might
be categorized as violent stool shifters.

c: Director, Science Lab
Director, NAS

Yes, more! →

Campus Communication

TO: All Parties in the L.A. "Stool-Shifting"
Controversy

FROM: A Concerned Male L.A. Stool Sitter

RE: A Plumbing Problem

I was relieved to learn that the water problem in the 2nd
Floor women's restroom has finally been flushed out.

The water seepage problem has long been an annoyance
in the men's restroom as well, and it now seems apparent
that the problem can be attributed to "Violent Stool
Shifters." I would hope that this insidious terrorist group
can be prevented from doing further damage to the
"underpinnings," as it were, of our society.

More! →

February 21

To: Dean Allen

From: Anonymous V.S.S.

I have been following the Saga of the Violent Stool Shifters with a great deal of interest, particularly because of my personal involvement with a problem of this type. I understand that you have suggested that one of your faculty members implement some sort of monitoring committee to identify the so-called perpetrators of this situation. I wish to express my dismay at this action.

Without revealing my identity, I would like to explain that I have been in contact with a number of persons who have been living with this behavior on a long-term basis. Recent studies seem to indicate that this is not an organic condition, but may be brought on by stress and/or poor diet, and is aggravated by general poor health. These people are victims, and should be given every opportunity to learn to deal constructively with their affliction. Public humiliation will only serve to drive them deeper into the closet, so to speak. It would be both humanitarian and productive for the administration to encourage the development of healthy attitudes among students and staff.

I would also like to see the development of a self-help group, something on the order of Alcoholics Anonymous, which would allow these people to reveal their identities to others who could encourage them in creating alternative life-styles. It is important thay they as individuals be allowed to live with dignity, no matter what their disability. I would be happy to be involved in the organization of this group.

Thank you for allowing me to express my feelings on this delicate and important issue. I, and others like me, are only seeking to live productive, dignified lives. Your understanding and encouragement will do much to promote healthier attitudes on campus and in the general public.

Still more! —>

Campus Communication

February 26

TO: Wendy Colton
             Science Lab

FROM: Jeffrey Allen, Dean, School of Arts and
             Sciences

RE: ABSOLUTE IMMEDIATE TERMINATION OF
             MONITORING OF VIOLENT STOOL SHIFTERS

The attached communication is self-explanatory. I deeply regret my insensitivity to the problems encountered by violent stool shifters.

Thank you.
Attachment

c: Director, Physical Plant

More! →

Campus Communication

February 28

TO: Jeffrey Allen, Dean, School of Arts & Sciences

FROM: Wendy Colton, Director, Science Lab

RE: VSS Task Force

I am in receipt of your memo and am relieved to be notified of the end of VSS responsibilities. Gathering data has been extremely difficult since this deep-seated problem seems to be transitive. On occasion, I have observed tremors and was unable to identify the individual because of the general overall wavelike behavior of the effects. In my attempt to determine the severity of the problem I had been using a Richter-type scale to differentiate between those VSS's who affected the seat condition and those who didn't.

I am grateful to be made aware, through your attached letter, of the origin and sensitivity of those poor souls afflicted with VSS Syndrome.

Among our original ideas we did include a voluntary self-help group for convicted offenders, and we will pursue this suggestion.

P.S. Do you have a use for 15,000 copies of the attached poster, since I now feel that they would be insensitive and inappropriate to disseminate from a plane over the campus? Thank you.

No more!

To: Whomever has been vandalizing the
           womens bathrooms

From: Director of Technical Services

Please consider that your actions create
unsanitary conditions for your co-workers, as
well as creating unnecessary work for the
cleaning service and Maintenance departments.

The other ladies that use and clean the restroom
would certainly appreciate it if you would stop
plugging up the toilets and causing them to
overflow all over the floors. It's offensive to
all of us.

Please think about what you are doing to your
peers. And think about whether putting your job
in jeopardy is worth it. This action warrants
immediate termination and when we identify the
individual(s), appropriate action will be taken.

"Individual(s)"? A conspiracy?

From: Department of General Services

To: ALL BUILDING TENANTS
             ALL EMPLOYEES
             ALL BUILDING CUSTODIANS

A thief is posing as a PLUMBER to get access to MEN'S ROOMS in various Government-type buildings. He carries a knapsack or canvas bag. He goes into stalls, shuts off the water, then removes, and steals the Flushometers.

Besides the cost of the flushometers, and the cost for our plumbers, there is also the inconvenience due to the downtime of the Mens Room.

We ask the cooperation of ALL employees. DGS plumbers will wear their City ID cards on their shirts. They are the only plumbers authorized to work in our bathrooms. If someone asked you for the combination to the men's room, or otherwise implies he is a plumber, look or ask for his ID card. If you hear someone working with wrenches in a stall, be cautious.

Call your Building Custodian if you are suspicious of such activities. Building Custodians have been advised to get assistance before trying to apprehend the thief.

Anyone wishing to offer information about this matter should contact our Security Office. Thank you for any cooperation.

Being New York, maybe a sign on the door, "No Flushometer" would work?

-6-

The

Apocryphal Now

W hat do "Mouseballs," "Restroom Trip
Bank," "New Travel Procedures," and
Tom Clancy have in common? They are
all among the most read non-Biblical literature of our time.
The first three are examples of apocryphal memos that have
spread through businesses, governments, and academia like
kudzu. They have been reproduced so often they have
achieved the status of artificial life; nonbiological organ-
isms which, amazingly, mutate very little from generation
to generation and so never evolve to a higher form of
literature.

Often humorous, sometimes taken for real, spreading
like viruses through e-mail systems, these zebra mussels of
the office pool may eventually crowd out more desirable
forms of business communication (should any exist),

forcing co-workers to actually talk to one another again, possibly about how the voice recognition system in the restrooms will work or where to get the best partially eaten meals while travelling.

They may not be real, but that doesn't mean they're not true.

Abstract: MOUSE BALLS NOW AVAILABLE AS FRU
(Field Replacement Unit)

Mouse balls are now available as FRU. Therefore, if a mouse fails to operate or should it perform erratically, it may need a ball replacement. Because of the delicate nature of this procedure, replacement of mouse balls should only be attempted by properly trained personnel.

Before proceeding, determine the type of mouse balls by examining the underside of each mouse. Domestic balls will be larger and harder than foreign balls. Ball removal procedures differ depending upon manufacturer of the mouse. Foreign balls can be replaced using the pop-off method, and domestic balls replaced using the twist-off method. Mouse balls are not usually static sensitive, however, excessive handling can result in a sudden discharge. Upon completion of ball replacement, the mouse may be used immediately.

It is recommended that each replacer have a pair of balls for maintaining optimum customer satisfaction, and that any customer missing his balls should suspect local personnel of removing these necessary functional items.

To order specify one of the following:

P/N 33F8462 - DOMESTIC MOUSE BALLS
P/N 33F8461 - FOREIGN MOUSE BALLS

Distributed everywhere as an "actual alert" to field engineers of a big computer power. It can't be real, but just in case, order P/N 33F8462 and tell me what you get.

TO: All Employees

FROM: GOVERNOR

DATE: DECEMBER 12

REGARDING: Employee Conduct

In the past, employees were permitted to make trips to the restroom under informal guidelines. Effective April 1, a Restroom Trip Policy (RTP) will be established to provide a consistent method of accounting for each employee's restroom time and ensuring equal treatment of all employees. This action is necessitated by marked increase in restroom privilege abuse.

Under this policy, a Restroon Trip Bank (RTB), will be established for each employee. The first day of each month, employees will be given a Restroom Trip Credit (RTC) of 20. Each time an employee uses the restroom, one trip credit will be deducted from his or her balance. Unused restroon trip credits may be accumulated from month to month, however, the balance may not exceed 30.

Currently, the entrances to all restrooms are being equipped with personal identification stations and computer-linked voice print recognition. During the next two weeks, each employee must provide two copies of voice prints (one normal; one under stress) to the personnel office. The voice print recognition station (VPRS) will be operated but not restrictive for the next two weeks. Employees should acquaint themselves with the stations during that period. Effective April 1, all VPRS will be fully activated and those potential restroom users without voice prints on file will be restricted from restroom use.

If an employee's Restroom Trip Bank (RTB) reaches zero, the door to all restrooms will not unlock for that employee's voice until the first day of the following month.

(continues)

In addition, the restrooms are being equipped with timed paper roll retractors (TPRR). If the restrooms is occupied for more than three minutes, an alarm will sound. Thirty seconds after the alarm sounds, the roll of paper in the restroom will retract. The toilet will flush, and the restroom door will automatically spring open.

If you have any questions, please contact your supervisor.

Next to "mouse balls," nothing has captured the working public's fancy like the restroom trip tank. They'd have to record your voice under stress for it to work.

THE TURBO-ALCOBULATOR

We have long been linked with scientific progress. Several world famous items developed into practical instruments. The Harger Drunkometer and the Borkenstein Breathalyzer are among the most notable.

The Instrument Division has periodically disseminated new scientific information in understandable terms. We thought it best to reprint the original text of the following article with its precise terminology.

The Turbo-Alcobulator is reprinted with permission of its author, J. H. Quick, B.Sc., London, England.

The Turbo-Alcobulator

For years work has proceeded to perfect the idea of an instrument that would not only supply inverse reactive current for use in unilateral phase detectors, but that would also automatically synchronize cardinal grammeters. Such a machine is the "Turbo-Alcobulator." The only new principle involved is that instead of power being generated by motion of fluxes it is produced by modial interaction of magneto-reluctance and capacitive directance.

The instrument has a base-plate of amulite, surmounted by a malleable casing so that two spurving bearings are in line with the pentametric fan. The latter consists of six hydrocoptic marzelvanes, fitted with an ambifacient waneshaft to prevent side-fumbling of the usual lotus-delta type panendermic slots. Every seventh conductor is connected to the girdlespring by a tremie pipe.

Forty-one manestic brushes feed the slip-stream with a mixture of S-phenylhydrobenzamine which has a pericosities of P + 2.5C where P is the diathetical evolute of retrograde

(continues)

temperature phase disposition and C is Cholmondeley's grillage coefficient. Initially, P was measured by a metapolar pilfrometer (see L.E. Rumpelstein in "Zeitschrift für Elektroteknisches-Donnerblitzen," vol. vii).

Early attempts to construct a spiral decommutator failed because of a lack of large quasi-piestic stresses in the gremlin studs; the latter were designed to hold the roffit bars so that wending could be prevented. Almost perfect running resulted.

The Turbo-Alcobulator has reached a high state of development. It has been successfully used for operating nofer tunnions. In addition, whenever a barescent skor is required, it may be employed in conjunction with a drawn dingle arm to reduce sinusoidal depleneration.

****

The giveaway here is the spurving bearings being in line with the penta-metric fan which would (in fact) shear off the hydro-coptic marzelvanes, stripping the manestic brushes, but you don't pick up on that the first time through.

REQUEST TO GET A LIFE

SEE SEPARATE INSTRUCTION FORM
THIS APPLICATION WILL NOT BE PROCESSED UNLESS ALL ITEMS ARE COMPLETED

1a. Name of Employe Requesting a "Life"   Phone

_____

Address

_____   County

City, Zip

_____

1.b Supervisor   Social Security
     Name(s)   Number(s)*

_____   _ _ _ - _ _ - _ _ _ _

_____   _ _ _ - _ _ - _ _ _ _

2. Employe Classification
   ☐ Sleezy Welfare Pimp (SWP)   ☐ Union Layabout (UL)
   ☐ Professional Leech (PL)   ☐ Janitor/Administrator (JA)
   ☐ High Muckety Muck (HMM)   ☐ Other (O)

3. When did you wish to "GET A LIFE"? (enter actual date)   _____

4. Do you ( ) have a life or ( ) don't have a life currently?
        If you have a life, describe why: _____

5. To be completed by SWP only.
                                                           Social Security
   Employe Name   Number*

_____   _ _ _ - _ _ - _ _ _ _

   Address
                                                           Phone
_____

   Amount you rip off from the poor (daily)   _____

6. To be completed by PL only
                                                           Social Security
   Employe Name   Number*

_____   _ _ _ - _ _ - _ _ _ _

   Reason for living

   I will ( ) will not ( ) wear a three piece suit to work
        Will ☐   Won't ☐

   Employee will be terminated if three piece suit is not worn

7. To be completed by HMM only.

   Name or Nickname   *Silly me. I filled out*

_____   *this form & was*
   Phone number in case of promotion *denied benefits.*

   President's Name
                                                           Social Security
_____   Number*

   Relation to Governor

_____   _ _ _ - _ _ - _ _ _ _

   Relation to Anyone Important

_____   _ _ _ - _ _ - _ _ _ _

* Social Security Numbers are not mandatory

TRYING TO DO THE JOB ALONE

Some of us have been guilty of trying to do the job alone while performing aircraft maintenance. This has resulted in dinged wing tips and tail fairings while moving aircraft and strained backs and mashed fingers while replacing components. Although costly, painful, and embarrassing, they are minor when compared to the following. May your consequences never be as severe as this person experienced.

Dear Sirs:

I am writing in response to your request for additional information. In block number three of the accident reporting form, I put "trying do the job alone" as the cause of my accident. You said in your letter that I should explain more fully, and I trust that the following details will be sufficient.

I am a bricklayer by trade. On the day of the accident, I was working alone on the roof of a new six-story building. When I completed my work, I discovered that I had about 500 pounds of brick left over. Rather than carry the bricks down by hand, I decided to lower them in a barrel by using a pulley which fortunately was attached to the side of the building at the sixth floor.

Securing the rope at ground level, I went up to the roof, swung the barrel out, and loaded the brick into it. Then I went back to the ground floor and untied the rope, holding it tightly to insure a slow descent of the 500 pounds of brick. You will note in block number 11 of the accident reporting form that I weigh 145 pounds.

Due to my surprise at being jerked off the ground so suddenly, I lost my presence of mind and forgot to let go of the rope. Needless to say, I proceeded at a rapid rate up the side of the building.

In the vicinity of the third floor, I met the barrel coming down. This explains the fractured skull and broken collarbone.

(continues)

Slowed only slightly, I continued my rapid ascent, not stopping until the fingers of my hand were two knuckles deep into the pulley. Fortunately by this time I had regained my presence of mind and was able to hold tightly to the rope in spite of my pain.

At approximately the same time, however, the barrel of bricks hit the ground, and the bottom fell out of the barrel. Devoid of the weight of the bricks, the barrel now weighed approximately 50 pounds.

I refer you again to my weight in block number 11. As you might imagine, I began a rapid descent down the side of the building.

In the vicinity of the third floor, I met the barrel coming up. This accounts for the two fractured ankles and the lacerations on my legs and lower body.

The encounter with the barrel slowed me enough to lessen my injuries when I fell onto the pile of bricks and, fortunately, only three vertebrae were cracked.

I am sorry to report, however, that as I lay there on the bricks, in pain unable to stand, and watching the empty barrel six stories above me, I again lost my presence of mind -- and I let go of the rope. The empty barrel weighed more than the rope so it came back down on me and broke both my legs.

I hope I have furnished the information you require as to how the accident occurred.

NOTE: Although amusing, this article makes painfully clear the seriousness of trying to do the job alone. Happy Holidays!

This gets a lot of Xerox play. It's been traced to Fred Allen (by one listener) and to an old Scottish folk ballad (by another).

NATIONAL BULLETIN NO. 205-0-21

SUBJECT: Travel-Changes in Government Policies
Concerning Meals and Accommodations

Purpose: To make employees aware of new travel policies
and procedures

Expiration
Date: September 30

Effective immediately the government has arranged for all
federal employees in travel status to make use of low-cost
quarters while traveling where government quarters are not
available.

The following changes are effective immediately:

1. Arrangements have been made to house federal
    employees in YMCA's and various public and correctional
    institutions available in most cities throughout the United
    States.

2. Employees on temporary duty to any city will be required
    to report to the local police department where they will
    receive an assignment to one of the many designated
    public housing facilities, possibly the local police station
    itself. If no quarters are available, employees on
    temporary duty will be issued a "statement of
    nonavailability". This will authorize employees on
    temporary duty to stay at a low-cost shelter for men or
    women in which adequate dormitory style facilities are
    available. Employees assigned to these facilities are
    advised to leave all personal belongings, shoes, etc. at
    the local police headquarters overnight.

3. Arrangements have been made with major airlines to
    make unused or partially eaten meals from previous

(continues)

flights available to government employees on temporary duty. These meals will be issued to travelers as they depart the aircraft and are to be eaten exclusively during the temporary duty period. All unused or uneaten meals are to be turned in by the traveler when boarding the return flight.

The above procedures are mandatory and will allow employees on temporary duty to stay within the GSA approved per diem rates and will eliminate the need for travel advances. Use of the Diners Club card when the participating lodging establishment will accept such is encouraged.

Employees in temporary duty status are reminded to park their government vehicles in a safe and secure parking area. If such parking arrangements are not available within walking distance, reimbursement is limited to bus fare.

While this trickled down through soil conservation in the USDA it can turn up anywhere—partially eaten meals are a perk.

I USED UP ALL MY
SICK DAYS SO I'M
CALLING IN
   " DEAD " ...
AND I'D LIKE 3
FUNERAL DAYS ALONG
WITH MY WEEKEND
OFF !!
            THANK YOU

He may not have said it first, he
may not have said it best, but this
ship steward said it in Marker!

MEMORANDUM

date: October 23

to: All Employees

from: The Donut Committee, Appeals Office

subject: OCCASIONS FOR DONUTS

From time to time (and the last time was August 10) it becomes necessary to restate the duties and responsibilities of all Appeals employees, as they relate to this office's unwritten rule about donuts. Due to the large influx of new Appeals employees, it behooves us once again to examine these unwritten policies.

The "bringing of the donuts" is an act unique to Appeals and heavily steeped in tradition. There are only a very few occasions in our lives which would require the "bringing of the donuts". Examples of "Required Donuts" are listed below.

In addition, there are other occasions of great personal joy and happiness which do not "require" donuts, _per se_, but for which donuts would be an appropriate vehicle for demonstrating one's joy and happiness. Over the years, numerous situations have prompted individuals to bring "Voluntary Donuts", and a list of those occasions is shown below. This list is not intended to be all-inclusive.

Other home-baked goodies may be substituted for donuts. The Donut Committee reserves the right to remind all employees of their duties and responsibilities.

The contents of this memorandum are not to be construed as constituting a written rule, only a reminder of an unwritten rule.

(continues)

Required Donuts	Voluntary Donuts
Birthday	In-Grades
Promotion	New Baby
Selection to Appeals	Grandchild
Retirement from Appeals	Selling a Home
Awards	Purchasing a Home
	Successful Surgery
	700 Series in Bowling
	300 Game
	Marriage
	Marriage of a Family Member
	Divorce (if appropriate)
	Winning Dog Sled Race

"Donuts, per se"? Hey, you can't tell me the IRS doesn't have a sense of humor.

Interoffice

To: Distribution

Location:

Answering: Eating In The Building

From: K. Tappis

Date: May 16

For the past two years we have been struggling with the problem of people eating in areas where chemical contamination of their food could pose health hazards. During recent months, OSHA has targeted lab hygiene in R & D facility inspections and issued citations for food consumption in lab and quasi lab areas including attached or adjoining office space.

At the May 9 managers meeting, the issue was discussed in detail and the management team reached the conclusion that the only practical means of dealing with this issue was to prohibit eating everywhere except the cafeteria and conference rooms.

Effective immediately, we are requesting that lunch and snacks be eaten in the specified areas. We realize that this may inconvenience some individuals but believe that the health and safety concerns justify the action.

Addenda:

1.   When the new facility is completed, it will have specified areas for the ingestion of non-toxic substances.

2a.   Since it is the intent of this policy to avoid the ingestion of toxic substances, the word "eating" shall be construed to include drinking. Hence, all consumption of coffee, tea, soft drinks, fruit juice, etc. is forbidden (except in the above-specified areas.)

(continues)

2b.　Consistent with this policy, the Maintenance Department has been instructed to remove all drinking water fountains at the earliest opportunity. Until such removal can be completed, all such fountains are off-limits.

3.　Since the fastest and most efficient way of introducing foreign substances into the body is by inhalation, all employees are hereby forbidden to breathe (except in the above-specified areas.) Strict adherence to this policy, with management setting an example for all of us, will result in a safer and happier workplace for everyone.

You know, he had me going right up to the "breathe" part.

Office Hours
for
U.S. Post Office
Council, # 42206

Open most days about 9 or 10.

Occasionaly as early as 7, but some days as late as 12 or 1. We close about 5^{30} or 6, Occasionaly about 4 or 5 but sometimes as late as 11 or 12. Somedays or afternoons we aren't here at all, and lately J've been here just about all the time, Except when J'm someplace else, But J should be here then, too.

J'd like to think the postmaster at this little post office in Virginia came up with this, but J'm just a hopeless romantic.

The Memo in

Space and Time

Something about a memo commands disrespect. When you consider how many memos have been written over the years, it's amazing how little attention has been paid to them, either individually or collectively, and yet they are the copper adzes and obsidian scrapers of our age. It's as if the Leakeys merely complained about all the bones littering their garden or as if, despite the billions and billions of stars, Carl Sagan never bothered to look up.

The urge to "memoize" is as old as mankind itself, or at least as old as the ability to write. When man first spoke, he must have realized what a vulnerable position it put him in and sought to devise a means by which he could distance himself by subordinating the trickier stuff and running things without standing in the field of fire. Memos would prove ideal.

The earliest memos were cuneiform things-to-remember incised on Sumerian wine pots and yanked, on donkeyback, to the far reaches of the pre-Babylonian empire for the instruction of field officers and administrators. (Some pots carried news from home; when dropped, they were late-breaking news.) The wine pots were a communications breakthrough in that they provided both a message and the means of forgetting it. The Sumerians were the prototypical bureaucrats whose development of a written language gave them unprecedented power, hindered only by the weight of their messages: In those days a stack of memos could fall over and crush you (the Sumerians never achieved a clayless workplace, but at least they had the satisfaction of being able to smash junk mail).

The weight problem was solved by the Egyptians and their papyrus, while the limited ability of pictographs to proclaim, threaten, and inveigh was finessed by the Phoenician invention of the alphabet. By 1200 B.C. everything was in place for modern memo dissemination except the carbon paper (but with labor costs low or nonexistent, a roomful of scribes was cost-effective) and the civil service.

Memo Milestones

3500 B.C.   Sumerian wine pot memos: one for the road.

2200 B.C.   Egyptian Abusir Papyri: cache of 2,000 memos detailing funerary rites for Pharaoh Raneferef.

1000 B.C.   Ten Commandments dictated, widely reproduced.

Third century B.C.   The Chinese establish the civil service, fertile breeding grounds for internal directives by unseen department heads.

553 A.D.   Monk Cassiodorus in Rome begins saving everything from receipts to ancient manuscripts. Advent of the illuminated memo.

1440   Johannes Gutenberg invents the printing press with movable type, opening up unlimited means of memo reproduction.

In 1465   a merchant named Paston asks, in a memorandum to Thomas More, that "because ye myzt foryete myne erand to Maister Bernay, I pray you rede hym my bille . . ." with no record of any response, at least not by *Utopia* (1516).

The *nota bene* sweeps Renaissance Italy; cousin to the French *notes verbales*, these are unsigned memos written in the third person, giving a latitude that memo writers can only dream of today.

In Shakespeare's *Henry IV*, Prince Hal upbraids Falstaff by telling him ". . . if there were anything in thy pocket but tavern-reckonings [and] memorandums of bawdy houses . . . I am a villain. . . ." "Memorandums" seems to refer to things to remember about the hostesses.

"God," according to Goad in his *Celestial Bodies* (1686) "hath imprinted on the Universe . . some Memorands or Signatures of His Creation," but just who received copies is unclear, despite claims made.

The first modern use of the memo as an essentially threatening written message to employees from a higher-up comes from Cornelius Vanderbilt to underlings in his steamship business: "Gentlemen: You have undertaken to cheat me. I won't sue you for the law takes too long. I will ruin you. Yours truly, . . ." To many, Vanderbilt's remains the epitome of effective business communication: a short and unambiguous call to action.

1873 The advent of the typewriter, first mass-produced by Remington, the gun maker; bullets soon yield to rapid-fire directives.

The memo's reputation as an insight into the real workings of an organization is established and preserved by Bell Telephone, as shown by this one, circa 1878, from the treasurer to the president (cited in Conference Board 70), recounting a conversation with a creditor:

> Mr. Cheever is I think sufficiently aware of our financial weakness not to make it desirable to any further enlighten him. I therefore went out of my way and told him a lie, that he might not think we were bankrupt. I hope I shall be pardoned for the number of highly colored statements I have been constantly obliged to make to keep up a semblance of financial solidity. We may and I trust will laugh over this one day but it is a sorry matter now. If I break down under it, deal gently with the widow and the fatherless!

Clearly, modern memo and management practices were up and running.

1890 Introduction of the manila folder.

1910 The words "From the desk of . . ." first appear.

1931 Movie Producer David O. Selznick begins an unbroken thirty-six years of Hollywood memos, including one to George Cukor on Clark Gable's refusal to affect a southern accent for Rhett Butler in *Gone with the Wind*.

1971   White House Counsel John Dean's "enemies list" memo prepared at the behest of President Nixon and saved at the behest of Dean.

1985   Oliver North writes a memo proposing air-dropping weapons to the Nicaraguan contras to help sink Sandinista ships. Marked "President approves."

1989   Bryant Gumbel writes in a memo that Willard Scott is holding the *Today Show* hostage to "birthdays . . . and bad taste."

1991   Microsoft chairman Bill Gates's memo to staff urging better performance; Microsoft stock drops ten percent in two days, resulting in $400 million paper loss for Gates alone.

1995   In a memo to Republican Congressmen delineating talking points on program cuts necessary for the Contract with America, pollster Frank Luntz advises "if we talk about *pain*, we lose. If we talk about a *better future*, we win.